Ribbons & Roses

32 Exquisite
Ribbon Embroidery Projects

LEE LOCKHEED

Guild of Master Craftsman Publications Ltd

For Richard, Sarah and Amy

First published in this paperback edition 1999
by Guild of Master Craftsman Publications Ltd
Castle Place, 166 High Street, Lewes,
East Sussex BN7 1XU

First published in Australia in 1998
by Tracy Marsh Publications Pty Ltd
PO Box 2075, Rose Bay North, NSW, 2030, Australia

Publisher: **Tracy Marsh**
Publishing Manager: **Jane Moseley**
Designer: **Vanessa Byrne**
Editor: **Leonie Draper**
Photographers: **Andre Martin, Joe Filshie**
Stylist: **Georgina Dolling**
Production Director: **Mick Bagnato**
Model: **Sophia Isabella Marsh Corbin**

Written and illustrated by Lee Lockheed
Technical diagrams by Kathy Barac

ISBN 186108 131 6

Manufactured by Phoenix Offset, Hong Kong
Printed in Hong Kong

Whilst all care is taken to provide the reader with knowledge of the safety precautions relating to the use of the
materials featured in this book, neither the Publisher, nor the Producer can take responsibility for personal injury
or mishap which may occur while working with the materials. Please read carefully all manufacturers' instructions
regarding the safe and effective use of materials and equipment before commencing work.

CREDITS
To the following individuals and companies the author would like to offer her sincere thanks for their assistance:
Kathy Barac for her continuing support and encouragement whilst compiling the book. Alan and Margaret
of Cotton on Creations, New South Wales, for supplying the silk ribbon. Christine of The Silk Company,
Linden Park, South Australia, for supplying the fabric for the baby layette projects. Bob and Nicki Martin, of Highbury,
South Australia, for the upholstery fabrics and constructing the heart and daisy cushions. The Smith Family
(The Mill Shop, Woodside, South Australia) for the wool blanketing. Lincraft (Adelaide) for donating fabric.
Sue Spork of Miller and Coates, Queensland, for donating the fabric, ribbon and braid for the burgundy rose cushion.
The publisher also wishes to thank the following companies (listed alphabetically) for providing items used in
this book: *Bed Bath n' Table; Flash Trash Antiques, Camperdown; Gradas Garden Florist; Home & Garden on the Mall;
Laura Ashley; Lincraft (Sydney); Seaview Christmas Decorations.*

Contents

Introduction

Throughout the centuries the popularity and styles of ribbon embroidery have constantly waxed and waned, reflecting the ever-changing and fickle trends of fashion.

Initially, extravagant and elaborate ribbon work was extensively used to embellish the costuming for both ladies and gentlemen of the aristocratic and well-to-do member of society.

Later, during the nineteenth century, as the popularity of ribbon embroidery grew, more practical items were decorated by a greater share of the population. Exquisitely embroidered mantle drapes and elegant cushions, enhanced with luxurious braids and tassels, graced the parlors and drawing rooms of Victorian homes. Accessories, including small silk bags for ladies, pin cushions, handkerchiefs, needle cases, and picture frames, featured smaller and more intricate flowers such as forget-me-nots, roses and daisies. These items were often made as gifts for friends and relatives, as a commemoration for a special occasion, or to be sold to earn money for the home or the local church.

The most commonly used ribbon of this time was 3mm (⅛") wide and was available in a variety of pretty colors, both shaded and plain. The ribbon makers of today are providing the embroiderer with an exciting array of breathtaking ribbons available in a myriad of textures and hues.

Cream on cream embroidery has always conjured up the essence of innocence, making it the perfect choice for the baby layette. Whilst working on the bows and the delicate sprays of the forget-me-nots on the baby's pram cover, I thought of how truly beautiful they would look embroidered on the bodice of a wedding dress (perhaps for one of my own daughters).

The selection of cushions, framed pieces and gifts, for you to make and treasure or give with love, employ a variety of ribbons ranging from the pure silks and satins through to the luxuriously flamboyant organdys. Beautifully frilled, piped, embroidered cushions, and pictures housed in ornate frames, can transform even the dowdiest of rooms, adding color, style, individuality and enormous charm.

Five embroidered woolen blankets, all adorned with ribbons and roses, adorable teddies and the traditional bluebirds for babies complete the projects of the book.

The designs are not only limited to ribbon or wool. For example the designs used in the Heritage Rose Blanket and Victorian Posy Rug, if worked in DMC cotton or Rajmahal, would look simply stunning on an elegant damask tablecloth.

Transform your bed linen by adding a stylish individual touch to pillow cases and the turn back of a special bed sheet. Create a lavish effect on curtain tie backs. Embroider white on white, or vary the rose colors to suit your own personal taste and decor.

The baby bear from the The Three Bears blanket can be used separately to make an adorable brooch for a little girl's special collar.

I hope that you will enjoy working with the gorgeous variety of ribbons that I have chosen and that this collection of original designs, patterns, diagrams and clear, concise instructions will tempt everyone, from the absolute beginner to the experienced embroiderer, to pick up a needle and create the many beautiful projects in Ribbons and Roses.

Happy stitching.

Lee Lockheed

BABY'S LAYETTE

*On a baby's Christening Day, in Victorian times,
the baby's appearance was considered to be of
the utmost importance. Elaborate gowns, jackets, bonnets
and booties, befitting a little prince or princess, were fashioned
in the finest cotton voiles or pure silk fabrics and adorned with tiny
tucking, laces and exquisite embroidery. Traditional gifts, such as
silver rattles, personalized Christening cups, coral and silver teething
rings, bracelets, lockets, bar brooches and small initialled
embroidered pillows or quilts were presented to the new baby
by doting grandparents, uncles and aunts.
Embroider the pieces in this Forget-me-not Baby Layette
for a much loved baby in your life.*

Forget-me-not
Baby's Jewelry Cushion

- silk satin-backed crepe (ivory)
- polyester filling
- 64cm (25") Russia Braid (ivory)
- 1m (39") silk ribbon, 4mm 156 (cream)
- Marlitt 1034 (ivory)
- Mill Hill Petite Glass Beads No. 40123
- sharp lead pencil
- embroidery hoop: 11.5cm (4½")
- pins & tape measure
- scissors
- needle & thread
- sewing machine

Stem Stitch Bow & Tails
Marlitt 1034

Straight Stitch Forget-me-not
Silk ribbon, 4mm 156

Bead Center
Petite Glass Beads 40123

Bullion Stitch Leaves
Marlitt 1034

Stem Stitch Stems
Marlitt 1034

Actual size

TO MAKE

Place a piece of the silk fabric, right side up, over the cushion pattern. Lightly trace the cushion outline and the embroidery design onto the fabric with a sharp lead pencil.

Using the embroidery hoop, embroider the design following the key as a guide.

Cut around the cushion outline. Cut a second piece of fabric, the same size as the first.

With right sides facing, machine stitch around the cushion, leaving an opening of about 6cm (2½").

Turn the cushion right side out and press lightly around the seams of the square. Slip stitch the opening closed.

Starting from the center front, slip stitch the Russia Braid around the edge of the cushion, looping the braid at the corners.

Forget-me-not
Baby's Coat Hanger

- silk satin-backed crepe (ivory):
  30cm x 40cm (11½" x 15½")
- poly-cotton poplin for lining
- medium-weight craft wadding:
  30cm x 40cm (11½" x 15½")
- small wooden coat hanger
- 15cm (6") satin bias binding (ivory)
- 60cm (23½") Russia Braid (ivory)
- 1m (39") silk ribbon, 4mm 156 (cream)
- Marlitt No. 1034 (ivory)
- Mill Hill Petite Glass Beads No. 40123
- sharp lead pencil
- embroidery hoop: 11.5cm (4½")
- pins & tape measure
- scissors
- needle & thread
- sewing machine

TO MAKE

All 1.5cm (⅝") seam allowances are included in the pattern on page 96.

With wrong sides facing, fold the satin-backed fabric in half lengthwise. Place the coat hanger pattern between the folded fabric pieces. Lightly trace the coat hanger outline and the embroidery design onto the fabric with a sharp lead pencil.

Place the fabric into the small embroidery hoop and embroider the design following the key as a guide.

Lightly press around the edge of the embroidery and cut out the front and back of the coat hanger.

Using the pattern and omitting the seam allowances, cut two pieces of wadding with the upper edge extending 6.5cm (2½") past the top stitch line on the pattern (diagram 1). Mark the top stitch line on both pieces of wadding.

Stitch the pieces of wadding together along the marked stitch line. Open the seam out flat. Unscrew the hook from the coat hanger. Fold the wadding over the coat hanger and tack the two pieces of wadding together directly below the hanger (diagram 2). Tack through all layers around the edge of the wadding.

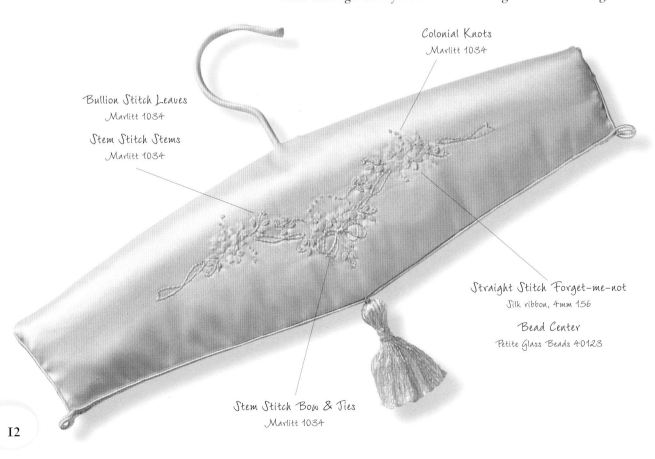

Colonial Knots
Marlitt 1034

Bullion Stitch Leaves
Marlitt 1034

Stem Stitch Stems
Marlitt 1034

Straight Stitch Forget-me-not
Silk ribbon, 4mm 156

Bead Center
Petite Glass Beads 40123

Stem Stitch Bow & Ties
Marlitt 1034

Actual size

Cut out the lining pieces. Place a piece of lining over the wrong side of the cover front and back. Tack the pieces together.

With right sides facing, tack the front and back together. Machine stitch the upper seam between the dots and press the seam open. Press under the seam allowance on the right-hand side of the cover. With right sides facing, machine stitch the lower seam between the dots (diagram 3).

Trim the seam, clip the lower corners and turn the cover right side out. Finger-press the lower seam.

Fold the seam allowance into the cover on the right-hand side. Fold the wadding up and slip the padded coat hanger through the opening in the side of the cover.

Carefully push the wadding in place to fit the shape of the cover. Slip stitch the opening, leaving a small hole at the top.

Make a length of rouleau using the satin bias. Before turning the rouleau right side out, stitch across one end.

Ease the rouleau over the wire hook. Screw the hook into the coat hanger, push the raw edges of the hook cover into the opening and slip stitch it closed.

Push the raw end of the Russia Braid though one of the small side openings and slip stitch the braid in place. Continue to slip stitch the braid around the coat hanger, looping it at each corner. Push the excess braid into the opening at the top of the seam and slip stitch to secure.

TO FINISH
To make the tassel, refer to Tassel Making instructions on page 85.

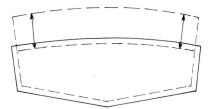

Diagram 1

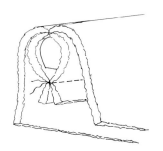

Diagram 2

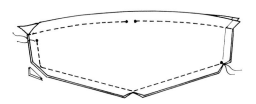

Diagram 3

Forget-me-not
Baby's Jacket

- silk satin-backed crepe, (ivory):
  70cm x 60cm (27½" x 23½")
- Paj silk lining, (ivory):
  70cm x 60cm (27½" x 23½")
- shirring elastic
- 60cm (23½") crepe Georgette ribbon,
  27mm No. 4546, No. 12 (ivory)
- 66cm (26") crepe Georgette ribbon,
  15mm, No. 4546, No. 12 (ivory)
- 2.5m (2¾ yds) silk ribbon, 4mm 156 (cream)
- Marlitt 1034 (ivory)
- Mill Hill Petite Glass Beads No. 40123
- sharp lead pencil
- embroidery hoop: 11.5cm (4½")
- pins & tape measure
- scissors
- needle & thread
- sewing machine

TO MAKE

Pattern size: newborn. All seam allowances of 1.5cm (⅝") are included in the pattern piece. Enlarge the pattern piece shown on page 97.

Fold fabric in half lengthwise, wrong sides facing.

Insert pattern piece between the pieces of the folded fabric so that the pattern fits firmly against the fold. Tack in place.

Lightly trace the embroidery design and the curve onto the left-hand side of the jacket front. Unpick the tacking and repeat for the right-hand side.

Using the small embroidery hoop, embroider the design following the key as a guide.

Fold the fabric in half, right sides facing. Pin the jacket pattern on the fold, aligning the pattern piece with the traced curve and embroidery.

Cut out the pattern piece, cutting up the fold for the front opening. Cut a second pattern piece to make the lining.

Attach 30cm (11¾") of 27mm Georgette ribbon on both sides of the jacket front, 1.5cm (⅝") down from the neck edge.

With right sides facing, stitch the arm and side seams together.

With right sides facing, stitch the lining to the jacket, omitting the sleeve edges and leaving a small opening of approximately 7cm (3") at the bottom of the jacket.

Turn right side out, press and slip stitch closed.

Tack the lining and jacket front together around the sleeve edges.

Sew two rows of shirring elastic 3cm (1¼") in from the sleeve edge.

Cut a piece of crepe Georgette 15mm ribbon to fit the sleeve. Fold in half and stitch to the sleeve edge, placing the join on the seam of the sleeve.

Bullion Stitch Leaves
Marlitt 1034

Stem Stitch Stems
Marlitt 1034

Stem Stitch Bows
Marlitt 1034

Straight Stitch
Forget-me-not
Silk ribbon, 4mm 156

Bead Center
Petite Glass Beads 40123

Forget-me-not
Baby's Romper

- 1.5m (59") silk satin-backed crepe (ivory)
- 1.5m (59") fine piping cord
- 1m (39") satin bias binding (ivory)
- 7 x 1cm (⅜") mother-of-pearl buttons
- 2 x 6mm (¼") mother-of-pearl buttons
- Marlitt No. 1034 (ivory)
- 30cm (11½") silk ribbon, 4mm 156 (cream)
- Mill Hill Petite Glass Beads No. 40123
- sharp lead pencil
- pins & tape measure
- scissors
- needle & thread
- sewing machine

TO MAKE

Pattern size: newborn. All 1.5cm (⅝") seam allowances are included in the pattern pieces.

Cut out the pattern pieces according to the cutting layout (see pages 98 and 99).

Pleat eight half space rows on the romper front. Smock according to the graph (shown this page).

Make up enough piping to cover the length of piping cord.

Cut a length of piping to fit the lower edge of the yoke. Pin and tack the piping to the right side of the romper front, aligning the stitch line slightly above the first cable row. Machine stitch in place (diagram 1).

Diagram 1

With right sides facing, pin and tack the front to the yoke front. Machine stitch in place.

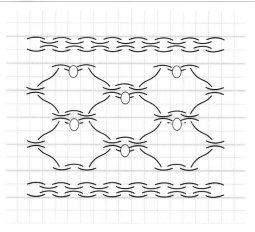

Stitch Key

Double cable just below pleating row 1.

Pleating rows 2—5: 4 rows of baby wave —3 cable combination.

Rows 2 and 4 are stitched as a mirror image of rows 1 and 3.

Double cable just above pleating row 6.

With right sides facing, stitch the center back seam to the dot. Clip to dot (diagram 2). Neaten and press the seam. Press the seam allowances on the continuous lap. With right sides facing, tack the lap to the back opening edges. Machine stitch in place (diagram 3). Press the lap out.

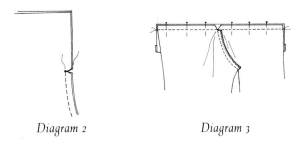

Diagram 2   *Diagram 3*

Tack the pressed edge of the lap over the seam. Slip stitch in place (diagram 4). Press the right-hand back edge to the inside and tack in place (diagram 5).

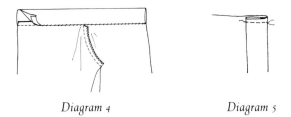

Diagram 4   *Diagram 5*

Stitch two gathering rows between the dots on the upper edge of the romper back sections. Pull up the gathering threads to fit the back yokes. With right sides facing, pin and tack the back yokes to the romper back pieces (diagram 6). Bring the back yoke lining over to the wrong side of the romper back. Tack. Machine stitch in place (diagram 7). Turn right side out and press.

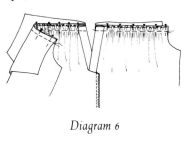

Diagram 6

Diagram 7

Stitch the front yoke to the back yokes at the shoulder seams. Repeat for the linings. Press the seams open (diagram 8).

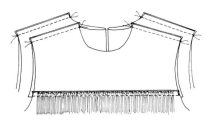

Diagram 8

Embroider the single flower from the pram quilt design, page 23, onto the collar pieces. Cut lengths of the piping to fit around the collar edges. Clip the heading. Matching the stitch lines, pin and tack the piping to the right side of the collar (diagram 9). With right sides facing, stitch the collar to the facing. Trim the seam to 3mm (⅛") (diagram 10). Turn the collar right side out and press.

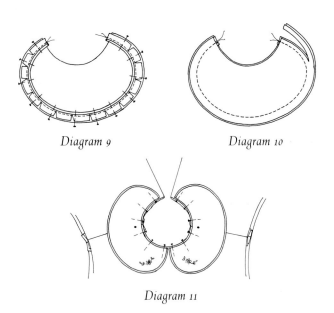

Diagram 9   *Diagram 10*

Diagram 11

Pin and tack the collar to the neck edge, matching the dots at the shoulders (diagram 11). Bring the linings to the right side, matching shoulder seams and center front, and tack in place. Machine stitch (diagram 12). Trim the seam and clip the curves. Turn right side out and press. Keeping the front and back yokes away from the linings, understitch around the neckline, 3mm (⅛") from the collar seam line. Tack the linings to the yokes around the armhole edges. Slip stitch the front yoke lining to cover the yoke seam.

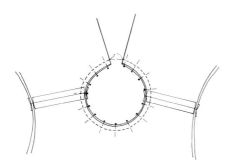

Diagram 12

Cut a length of piping to fit across the lower edge of each sleeve. Matching stitch lines, pin and tack piping to the right side of each sleeve. Machine stitch in place. Press the seam allowance on one side of each cuff. With right sides facing, stitch the cuffs to the sleeves (diagram 13). Trim the seam and press the cuff and seam downwards.

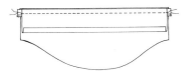

Diagram 13

Stitch two gathering rows across the head of each sleeve between the dots. With right sides facing and matching the dots, pin the sleeve into the armhole.

Pull up the gathers to ease the sleeve into place. Machine stitch (diagram 14). Trim and neaten seam.

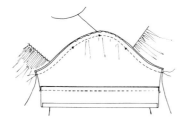

Diagram 14

With right sides facing and matching the underarm seams, pin and tack the front to the back along sides. Machine stitch (diagram 15). Trim and neaten seam. Press. Fold the lower edge of the cuffs to the inside and slip stitch along the seam line (diagram 16).

Cut a length of the satin binding to fit the front and back inner leg seams. With right sides facing and matching stitch lines, stitch the binding along the inner leg seam.

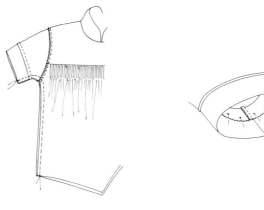

Diagram 15   *Diagram 16*

Press the binding out. Turn to the wrong side and machine stitch in place.

Stitch two gathering rows across the lower leg edge between the dots. Cut a length of piping to fit each leg cuff. With right sides facing, pin and tack piping across one edge of each cuff. Press under the seam allowance on the opposite edge of the cuff.

With right sides facing, pin the piped edge of the cuff at both ends of the lower leg. Pull up the gathering threads to fit. Pin and tack. Machine stitch in place (diagram 17). Press the cuff downwards.

Diagram 17

With right sides facing, bring the lower edge of the cuff up to meet the piped seam line. Machine stitch across both ends.

Clip the corner and turn right side out. Slip stitch in place along the seam line (diagram 18). Press.

Diagram 18

TO FINISH

Work the buttonholes on the front inner legs and the back yoke as shown on the pattern pieces. Sew the buttons in place.

Forget-me-not
Baby's Booties

- silk satin-backed crepe (ivory)
- iron-on interfacing
- 1.15m (45") satin binding (ivory)
- 40cm (16") crepe Georgette ribbon, 15mm No. 4546 (ivory)
- 2m (78") silk ribbon, 4mm 156 (cream)
- Marlitt 1034 (ivory)
- Mill Hill Petite Glass Beads, No. 40123
- sharp lead pencil
- embroidery hoop: 11.5cm (4½")
- pins & tape measure
- scissors
- needle & thread
- sewing machine

TO MAKE

Pattern size: newborn. All 6mm (¼") seam allowances are included in the pattern.

Place a piece of the satin-backed fabric, 18cm x 22cm (7" x 8½") right side up over the shoe pattern. Lightly trace the shoe outline and the embroidery design onto the fabric with a sharp lead pencil. Trace the sole pattern piece in the space above the shoe upper.

Using the embroidery hoop, embroider the design, following the key as a guide.

Press around the edge of the embroidery and cut out the shoe upper and sole pattern pieces.

Cut a second piece of the fabric and a piece of soft iron-on interfacing 18cm x 22cm (7" x 8½"). Iron the interfacing onto the back of the fabric.

Tack the embroidered shoe upper and sole right sides facing onto the fabric. Cut around the shoe and sole outlines and unpick the tacking.

With right sides facing, stitch a 5mm (¼") back seam on the lining and the shoe upper. Turn right side out and press seams.

Tack the top of the lining and the embroidered uppers together, right sides facing, and sew a seam 3mm (⅛") wide.

Turn right side out, press and tack the lining and shoe front together around the bottom of the uppers.

Cut a piece of satin binding to fit around the bottom of the shoe upper. Trim away the folded edge on one side of the satin binding. With right sides facing, tack the cut edge of the satin binding around the bottom of the shoe upper, placing the join at the center back. Machine sew a 5mm (¼") seam around the satin binding. Trim seam, press, fold satin binding over to the back of the shoe upper and hand stitch the binding in place.

With wrong sides facing, tack the sole fabric pieces together. Cut a piece of satin binding to fit around the edge of the sole. Trim away folded edge on one side of the satin binding. With right sides facing, tack the cut edge of the satin binding around the edge of the sole. Join the binding at the center back and machine stitch a 5mm (¼") seam around the sole.

Trim seam, press, fold satin binding over to the back of the sole, hand stitch in place and press.

Turn the shoe upper inside out with wrong sides facing and slip stitch the sole to the shoe by joining the satin binding of the shoe upper and sole together. Turn shoe right side out.

Fold the crepe Georgette ribbon in half, sew it around the top of the shoe and tie a bow.

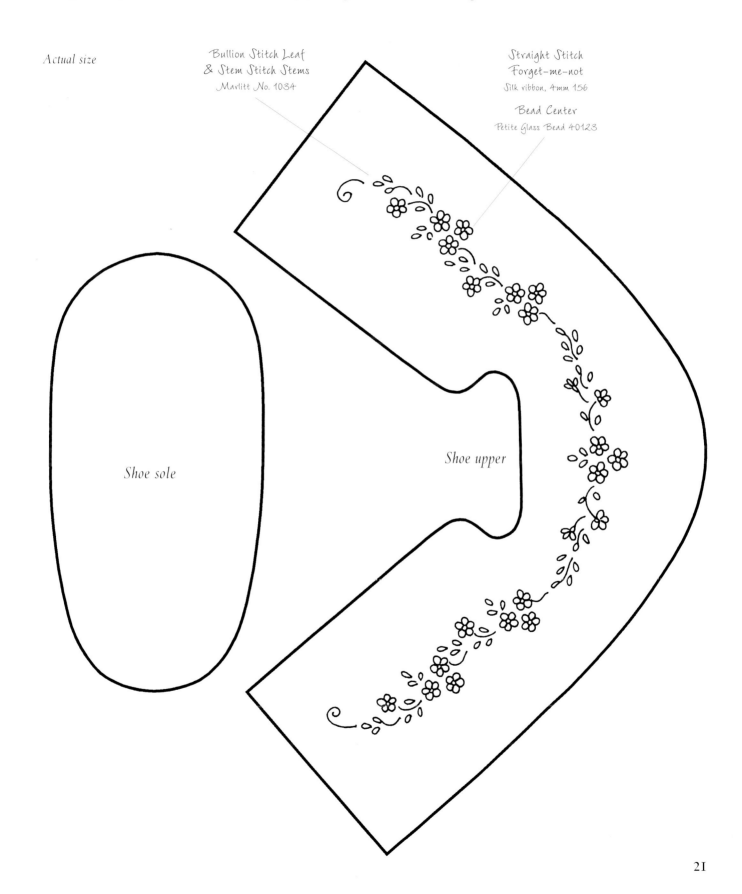

Actual size

Bullion Stitch Leaf & Stem Stitch Stems
Marlitt No. 1034

Straight Stitch Forget-me-not
Silk ribbon, 4mm 156

Bead Center
Petite Glass Bead 40123

Shoe sole

Shoe upper

Forget-me-not
Baby's Pram Quilt

- 1.5m (1⅔ yds) silk satin-backed crepe (ivory)
- pure wool wadding: 63cm x 47cm (24½" x 18½")
- 15m (16½ yds) silk ribbon, 4mm 156 (cream)
- Marlitt No. 1034
- Mill Hill Petite Glass Beads 40123 (pearl)
- sharp lead pencil
- pins & tape measure
- scissors
- needle & thread
- sewing machine

Forget-me-not
Silk ribbon, 4mm 156

Bead Center
Petite Glass Bead 40123

Bullion Stitch Leaves
Marlitt 1034

Stem Stitch Stems
Marlitt 1034

Stem Stitch Bow
Marlitt 1034

TO MAKE

All seam allowances are 1.5cm (⅝").

Cut two pieces of fabric, front and back of cover, 63cm x 47cm (24½" x 18½").

Cut one piece of lining 63cm x 47cm (24½" x 18½").

Cut four strips of fabric 14cm x 115cm (5½" x 45") to make the frill.

Trace the pattern shown below. Place the cover front right side up over the pattern. Using a sharp lead pencil, lightly trace the design onto the fabric.

Embroider the cover using the key as a guide.

Tack the wool wadding, the lining and the cover front together. Neaten raw edges.

Stem stitch in Marlitt around the border of the embroidery design, stitching through all layers of the fabric, including the wool wadding.

With right sides facing, join the frill strips into a continuous length. Press the seams open.

With wrong sides facing, fold the frill in half lengthwise.

Neaten raw edges and stitch two gathering rows 15mm (⅝") in from the edge of the frill.

Pull up the gathers to fit the cover front, pin and tack. Machine stitch in place.

Neaten the raw edges of the cover back.

With right sides facing, pin and tack the back to the cover front. Machine stitch in place leaving a small side opening of approximately 12cm (4½").

Turn right side out and slip stitch the opening.

Actual size

Forget-me-not
Baby's Blanket

- flannel blanketing (cream):
  100cm x 70cm (39" x 27½")
- flannel blanketing (cream):
  76cm x 53cm (30" x 21")
- 4.2m (4⅔ yds) cotton lace, 3cm (1¼")
- 4m (4⅓ yds) cotton lace beading
- 4.2m (4⅔ yds) silk ribbon, 7mm 156 (cream)
- 6m (6½ yds) silk ribbon, 4mm 156 (cream)
- DMC Broder Medicis—ecru
- Marlitt 1034 (ivory)
- Mill Hill Petite Glass Beads 40123
- fabric marking pen
- pins & tape measure
- scissors
- needle & thread
- sewing machine

TO MAKE

The pattern for the blanket is shown on page 100. Trace and cut out the scalloped corners of the center blanket piece using the Wild Pansy Bed Jacket corner template on page 107.

Buttonhole stitch with one strand of Medicis ecru around the scalloped and straight edges of the center blanket piece.

Embroider using the key as a guide. Using one strand of Marlitt 1034, embroider the bullion leaves by working eight twists on one side of the leaf and ten twists on the other.

Tack the center blanket onto the larger blanket. Using one strand of Marlitt 1034, stem stitch through all the layers around the edge of the buttonhole stitch, joining the blanket pieces.

TO FINISH

The blanket has been finished with a lace edging as used on the Victorian Posy Rug (refer to page 75). Using one strand of Marlitt 1034, stem stitch around the edge of the lace beading.

Bullion Stitch Leaves
Marlitt 1034

Stem Stitch Stems
Marlitt 1034

Satin Stitch Bows
DMC Medicis ecru

Straight Stitch Forget-me-not
Silk ribbon, 4mm 156

Bead Center
Petite Glass Beads 40123

Increase tracing to 238%

CUSHIONS

*Cushions represent the feminine touch in life.
They are soft and pretty, decorative and comfortable.
Beautiful, handmade cushions tell the world that this
house is also a home and that someone has taken the time
and trouble to add welcome homely touches.
This selection of ribbons and roses cushions will inspire you to
create your own cushions to suit your home and your mood or to give
as gifts to the ones you love.*

Gold Heart Cushion

- 40cm x 115cm (15½" x 45") gold satin-backed twill
- 50cm x 115cm (19½" x 45") burgundy organza
- 80cm x 115cm (31½" x 45") gold organza
- 50cm (19½") burgundy satin-backed twill for piping
- cushion filling
- 1.2m (48") piping cord
- 2m (2½ yds) silk ribbon, 7mm, 163 & 157 (pink)
- 2m (2½ yds) silk ribbon, 13mm 129 (burgundy)
- 3m (3⅓ yds) silk ribbon, 4mm, 179 (purple), 178 (purple), 53 (yellow), 171 (dark green), 56 (green)
- DMC cottons: 610 (green), 310 (black), 680 (gold), 315 (burgundy), 316 (pink)
- masking tape
- pins & tape measure
- scissors
- needle & thread
- sewing machine

Bullion Stitch Rose Buds
DMC cotton 316

Ribbon Roses
Silk ribbon, 13mm 129

Ribbon Rose Bud
Silk ribbon, 7mm 163

Colonial Knot Wisteria
Silk ribbon, 4mm 178, 179

Straight Stitch Calyx
Silk ribbon, 4mm 56

Ribbon Stitch Leaves
Silk ribbon, 4mm 171

Colonial Knots
DMC cotton 315

Straight Stitch Black-eyed Susan
Silk ribbon, 4mm 53

Stem Stitch Stems
DMC cotton 610

Colonial Knot Center
DMC cotton 310

Tea Roses
Silk ribbon, 7mm 163
Silk ribbon, 7mm 157

Satin Stitch Leaves
Silk ribbon, 4mm 171, 56

Satin Stitch Black-eyed Susan Buds
DMC cotton 680

Satin Stitch Rose Buds
DMC cotton 315

Satin Stitch Calyx Stem Stitch Stems
DMC cotton 610

Satin Stitch Calyx
DMC cotton 610

TO MAKE

All seam allowances are 1.5cm (⅝").

Enlarge the heart template (page 101) and, using the key as a guide, embroider the cushion front.

Join the 5cm (2") wide fabric strips into a single length to cover the piping cord. Place the piping cord down the center of the wrong side of the strip, fold over the piping cord, machine stitch with zipper foot.

Square off one end and pin the piping to the front piece of the cushion, starting half way along one side and continuing to the first corner. Clip the piping fabric and fold the piping around the corner of the cushion. Pin the piping around the rest of the cushion front until you reach your starting point.

Cut off excess piping, allowing 1.5cm (⅝") extra at ends. Unpick stitching up to 4cm (1½") at both ends.

With right sides facing, machine stitch the ends of the fabric together. Press the seam open.

Trim 1.5cm (⅝") from both ends of the piping cord.

Butt the cut ends together and wrap the join with masking tape. Place the piping cord back inside the fabric and stitch again. Using a zipper foot, machine stitch the piping to the cushion front.

Cut three widths of gold organza and three of burgundy for the frills. With right sides facing, join three fabric strips into a continuous length.

Fold frill in half lengthwise, wrong sides facing, and stitch two gathering rows along the raw edge.

Pin the frill evenly around the cushion front. Pull up the gathers, allowing extra at each corner. Pin and machine stitch the frill to the cushion front.

Cut cushion back using the enlarged heart template. Pin and tack the cushion back to the cushion front, leaving an opening of 15cm (6"). Machine stitch in place. Clip around the heart edge and neaten the raw edges. Turn right-side out. Fill the cushion and slipstitch the opening closed.

For more information see Cushion Making page 92.

Ring of Roses Cushion

Extended Pistol
Stitch Flower
DMC cotton 680

Colonial Knot Flower
Silk ribbon, 4mm 156

Stem Stitch Stem
DMC cotton 611

Ribbon Stitch
Wild Rose
Rayon ribbon 12

Extended Pistol
Stitch Stamen
DMC cotton 680

Satin Stitch Leaves
Stem Stitch Stems
DMC cotton 611

- 1.5m x 1.15m (1⅓ yds x 45") cream silk
- 30cm (11½") matching zipper
- 3m (3⅓ yds) Pan Pacific organdy ribbon, 24mm SN 1083, No. 11 (green)
- 1m (39") Makuba crepe Georgette ribbon, 15mm No. 4546, No. 00 (white)
- 1m (39") Makuba rayon ribbon, 13mm No. 1505, No. 12 (white)
- 2m (2½ yds) Makuba rayon ribbon, 13mm No. 1505, No. 14 (gold)
- 1m (39") double-faced satin ribbon, 9mm (cream)
- 1m (39") organdy ribbon, 24mm (white)
- 3m (3⅓ yds) silk ribbon, 4mm 156 (cream)
- DMC cottons: 680 (gold), 611 (green)
- pins & tape measure
- scissors
- needle & thread
- sewing machine

TO MAKE

All seam allowances are 1.5cm (⅝").

Make four ribbon roses by placing the rayon ribbon (No. 14) on top of the organdy ribbon (No. 11) and fold them together.

Make four ribbon roses by placing the rayon ribbon (No. 12) on top of the organdy ribbon (white) and fold them together.

Make four ribbon roses of crepe georgette, four smaller roses of double-faced satin and four of rayon ribbon (No. 14).

Make twenty eight ribbon leaves of organdy ribbon (No. 11).

Embroider the design (see page 102) onto the cushion front using the key as a guide. Sew the roses and leaves in place.

Cut four widths of cream silk for the frill. With right sides facing, sew a single length from the four silk strips. With wrong sides facing, fold the frill in half lengthwise. Stitch two gathering rows along the raw edge of the frill.

Pin the frill evenly around the cushion front. Pull up the gathers, allowing extra at each corner. Pin and machine stitch the frill to the cushion front.

Cut two pieces, each 36cm x 19.5cm (14" x 7¾"). With right sides facing, stitch the pieces together for a distance of 2.5cm (1") from each end. Press the seam open.

With the right side of the zipper facing the wrong side of the fabric, position the zipper behind the opening. Pin and machine stitch the zipper in place. Press the completed cushion back.

Open the zipper and, with right sides facing, pin and tack the cushion back to the cushion front, keeping the frill clear of the seam. Machine stitch, clip the corners and neaten the raw edges. Turn through to the right side.

Using two strands of DMC cotton 680, work a stem stitch around the cushion front, close to the frill.

For more information (and diagrams) refer to the section on Cushion Making on page 92.

Daisy Cushion

- 1.3m x 1.15m (51" x 45") green and white checked upholstery fabric
- 50cm (19½") white fabric for piping
- 1.5m (1⅓ yds) piping cord
- 30cm (11½") matching zipper
- 5m (5½ yds) silk ribbon, 7mm 156 (cream)
- 4m (4⅓ yds) silk ribbon, 4mm, 171 (dark green), 56 (green)
- 1m (39") silk ribbon, 4mm 156 (cream)
- DMC cottons: 422 (yellow), 3012 (green), 612 (green), 420 (brown)
- masking tape
- pins & tape measure
- scissors
- needle & thread
- sewing machine

Straight Stitch Bud
Silk ribbon, 4mm 156

Straight Stitch Calyx
Silk ribbon, 4mm 56

Straight Stitch Daisy
Silk ribbon, 7mm 156

Colonial Knot Center
DMC cottons 422, 3012

Satin Stitch Leaves
Silk ribbon, 4mm 171, 56

Stem Stitch Center
DMC cotton 420

Stem Stitch Stems
DMC cotton 612

TO MAKE

All seam allowances are 1.5cm (⅝").

Cut out the pieces, referring to the Cutting Layout shown on page 94. Embroider the design (see page 103) onto the cushion front using the key as a guide.

Join the fabric strips, which are 5cm (2") wide and cut on the cross, into a length sufficient to cover the piping cord. Place the piping cord down the center of the wrong side of the fabric strip. Fold fabric over the piping cord, machine stitch using zipper foot.

Square off one end and pin the piping to the front piece of the cushion, starting half way along one side and continuing to the first corner. Clip the piping fabric and fold it around the corner of the cushion. Continue to pin the piping around the cushion front until you reach your starting point. Cut off excess piping, allowing 1.5cm (⅝") extra at ends. Unpick the piping stitching up to 4cm (1½") at both ends.

With right sides facing, machine stitch the ends of the fabric together. Press the seam open.

Trim 1.5cm (⅝") from both ends of the piping cord. Butt the cut ends together and wrap the join with masking tape. Place the piping cord back inside the fabric and stitch again. Using a zipper foot, machine stitch the piping to the cushion front.

If using an upholstery fabric, cut three widths for the frill. With right sides facing, join three fabric strips into a continuous length.

Fold the frill in half lengthwise, wrong sides facing. Stitch two gathering rows along the raw edge.

Pin the frill evenly around the cushion front. Pull up the gathers, allowing extra at each corner. Pin and machine stitch the frill to the cushion front.

Cut two pieces 36cm x 19.5cm (14" x 7¾"). With right sides facing, stitch the pieces together for 2.5cm (1") from each end. Press seam open.

With right side of zipper facing wrong side of fabric, pin the zipper behind the opening. Machine stitch in place. Press the completed cushion back.

Open the zipper and, with right sides facing, pin and tack cushion back to cushion front, keeping the frill clear of the seam. Machine stitch, clip the corners and neaten the raw edges. Turn through.

For more information (and diagrams) refer to the section on Cushion Making on page 92.

Burgundy Rose Cushion

- 1.5m x 1.15m (1⅛ yds x 45") burgundy silk
- 1.3m (51") matching fringe braid
- 30cm (11½") matching zipper
- 3.5m (3 yds 30") Makuba organdy ribbon, 75mm No. 4563, No. 4 (burgundy)
- 2m (2½ yds) Makuba luminous ribbon, 13mm No. 4599, No. 5 (green)
- pins & tape measure
- scissors
- needle & thread
- sewing machine

Ribbon Roses
Organdy ribbon, 75mm No. 4

Bud
Organdy ribbon, 75mm No. 4

Ribbon Leaves
Luminous ribbon, 13mm No. 5

TO MAKE

All seam allowances are 1.5cm (⅝").

Using the organdy ribbon, make one large ribbon rose, two slightly smaller roses, and three rose buds.

Sew the large ribbon rose and the two smaller ribbon roses together in a bunch.

Attach the ribbon leaves to each ribbon rose bud and tie them to the roses.

Bring a piece of luminous ribbon up through the center of the cushion and use it to tie the bunch of ribbon roses onto the cushion.

Cut four widths of the burgundy silk fabric for the frill. With right sides facing, join the four fabric strips into a single continuous length.

With wrong sides facing, fold the frill in half lengthwise. Stitch two gathering rows along the raw edge of the frill.

Pin the frill evenly around the cushion front. Pull up the gathers, allowing extra fabric at each corner.

Pin the frill to the front of the cushion and machine stitch it in position.

Cut two pieces 36cm x 19.5cm (14" x 7¾"). With right sides facing, stitch the two pieces together for a distance of 2.5cm (1") from each end. Carefully press the seam open.

With the right side of the zipper facing the wrong side of the fabric, position the zipper behind the opening. Pin and machine stitch the zipper in place using a zipper foot. Press the completed back section of the cushion.

Open the zipper and, with right sides facing, pin and tack the cushion back section to the cushion front, taking care to keep the frill well clear of the seam. Machine stitch, clip all the corners and neaten the raw edges.

Turn the cushion right side out. Hand stitch the braid to the cushion front.

For more information (and diagrams) refer to the section on Cushion Making on page 92.

Old Gold Rose Cushion

- cream upholstery fabric for cushion front, back and piping (refer to Cutting Layout on page 94.)
  - 1.2m (48") piping cord
  - 30cm (11½") matching zipper
  - 1 x 28mm self-cover button
  - 1m (39") Makuba organdy ribbon, 15mm No. 1520, No. 49 (gold)
  - 7m (7½ yards) Makuba rayon ribbon, 13mm No. 1505, No. 14 (gold)
  - 5m (5½ yards) Makuba rayon ribbon, 6mm No. 1505, No. 16 (green)
  - DMC cotton: 640 (green)
  - masking tape
  - fabric marking pen
  - pins & tape measure
  - scissors
  - needle & thread
  - sewing machine

Ribbon Curves
Rayon ribbon 14

Chain Stitch Base
DMC cotton 640

Tea Rose
Rayon ribbon 13mm No. 14
Organdy ribbon 15mm No. 49

Ribbon Stitch Leaves
Rayon ribbon 6mm No. 16

Stem Stitch Stems
DMC cotton 640

Straight Stitch Rose
Rayon ribbon 6mm No. 16

Buds & Calyx
Rayon ribbon 13mm No. 14

TO MAKE

All seam allowances are 1.5cm (⅝").

Mark the curved lines of the design (see page 104) onto the cushion front. Chain stitch over the lines using six strands of DMC cotton (green). Whip over the chain stitch with Makuba rayon ribbon No. 14 (gold).

Using the embroidery design as a guide, work the four main tea roses, buds, leaves and stems.

Join the fabric strips, which are 5cm (2") wide and cut on the cross, into a continuous length sufficient to cover the required piping cord. Place the piping cord down the center of the wrong side of the fabric strip. Fold the fabric to enclose the piping cord and machine stitch, using a zipper foot.

Square off one end and pin the piping to the front piece of the cushion, starting half way along one side and continuing to the first corner. Clip the piping fabric and fold the piping around the corner of the cushion. Continue pinning the piping in this manner until you reach your starting point.

Cut off the excess piping, allowing 1.5cm (⅝") extra at both ends. Unpick the piping stitching up to 4cm (1½") at both ends.

With right sides facing, machine stitch the ends of the fabric together. Press the seam open.

Trim 1.5cm (⅝") from both ends of the piping cord. Butt the cut ends together and wrap the join with masking tape. Place the piping cord back inside the fabric and stitch again. Using a zipper foot, machine stitch the piping to the cushion front.

Cut two pieces 36cm x 19.5cm (14" x 7¾"). With right sides facing, stitch the two pieces together for 2.5cm (1") from each end. Press seam open.

With the right side of the zipper facing the wrong side of the fabric, position the zipper behind the opening. Pin and machine stitch the zipper in place. Press the completed cushion back.

Open the zipper and, with right sides facing, pin and tack the cushion back to the cushion front. Machine stitch, clip the corners and neaten the raw edges. Turn right side out.

For more information refer to page 92.

FRAMED PIECES

Your needlework achievements can be displayed as true works of art when you create these pieces and have them framed to be hung on the wall or placed on a mantlepiece. These designs will allow your skills plenty of scope for display. All of these beautiful works can take pride of place in the finest homes.

Rose Garland

- ivory silk with painted rose center
  (see Materials, page 84)
- 3m (3⅓ yds) silk ribbon, 7mm 163 (pink)
- 3m (3⅓ yds) silk ribbon, 4mm 158 (pink)
- 5m (5½ yds) silk ribbon, 4mm, 157 (pink), 163 (pink)
- 4m (4⅓ yds) silk ribbon, 4mm,
  171 (dark green), 56 (green)
- DMC cottons: 936 (dark green), 3013 (green)
- Mill Hill Petite Glass Beads No. 40557 (gold)
- gold metallic thread
- 8 small pearls
- embroidery hoop: 22cm (8½")
- soft wadding
- pins & tape measure
- scissors
- needle & thread

TO MAKE

Embroider the garland using the key as a guide.

Measure and cut a piece of soft wadding to fit the piece.

The finished piece and the wadding must be stretched on a mat board before being mounted. Unless you are experienced at framing embroidery pieces, take the finished work to a professional framer, and select a frame and mount to suit both the piece and its eventual display position in the home.

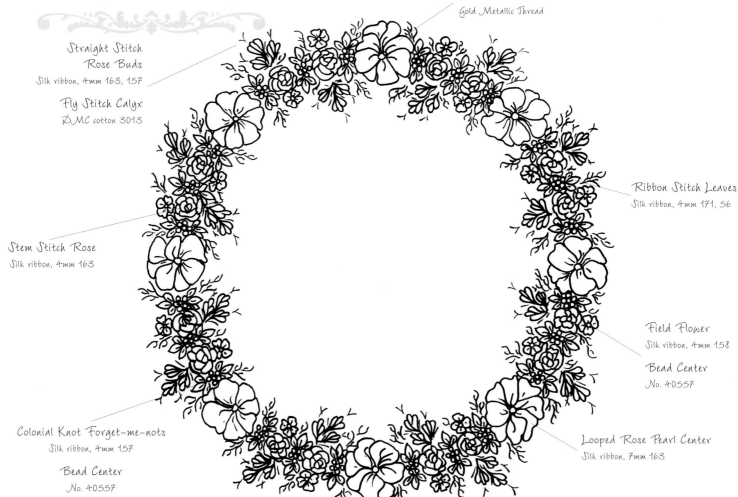

Fly Stitch Leaves
DMC cottons 936, 3013
Gold Metallic Thread

Straight Stitch
Rose Buds
Silk ribbon, 4mm 163, 157

Fly Stitch Calyx
DMC cotton 3013

Ribbon Stitch Leaves
Silk ribbon, 4mm 171, 56

Stem Stitch Rose
Silk ribbon, 4mm 163

Field Flower
Silk ribbon, 4mm 158

Bead Center
No. 40557

Colonial Knot Forget-me-nots
Silk ribbon, 4mm 157

Bead Center
No. 40557

Looped Rose Pearl Center
Silk ribbon, 7mm 163

Increase tracing to 117%

Rose Cherub

Ribbon Roses
Striped Organdy ribbon, 15mm, No. 14
Metallic Satin ribbon, 15mm, No. 34
Organdy ribbon, 15mm, No. 31

Colonial Knots
DMC cotton 680

Extended Pistol Stitch
DMC cottons 224, 315

Ribbon Leaves
Luminous ribbon, 13mm, No. 5
Organdy ribbon, 24mm, No. 11

Ribbon Bows
Striped Organdy ribbon, 8mm, No. 14

Actual size

- gold embossed upholstery fabric
- hand-painted metal cherub
- 1m (39") striped organdy ribbon
  No. 4597, 8mm, No. 14 (blue-gold)
- 30cm (12") Makuba striped organdy ribbon
  No. 4597, 15mm, No. 14 (blue-gold)
- 50cm (20") Makuba metallic satin ribbon
  No. 4934, 15mm, No. 34 (gold)
- 50cm (20") Makuba organdy ribbon
  No. 1520, 15mm, No. 31 (pink)
- 50cm (20") Makuba luminous ribbon
  No. 4599, 13mm, No. 5 (green)
- 50cm (20") Pan Pacific organdy ribbon
  No. 1083, 24mm, No. 11 (green)
- DMC cottons: 224 (pink), 315 (burgundy),
  680 (gold)
- soft wadding
- pins & tape measure
- scissors
- needle & thread

TO MAKE

Sew the cherub in place onto the fabric.

Make two ribbon roses of stripe organdy ribbon (15mm), three of metallic satin ribbon and three of the organdy ribbon.

Make eight ribbon leaves by placing the luminous ribbon on top of the green organdy ribbon and fold together.

To work the extended pistol stitch flowers, thread the needle with one strand of pink and one of burgundy DMC cotton.

Using the design and the key (shown above) as guides, sew the roses, leaves, and bows in place. Anchor the bow tails with colonial knots.

Measure and cut a piece of soft wadding to fit the completed piece.

The finished piece must be stretched before being mounted in a raised mat. Unless you are experienced at framing embroidery pieces, take the finished work to a professional framer, and select a frame and mount to suit both the piece and its eventual display position in the home.

The finished embroidery will need to be recessed within the frame.

Cameo Garland

TO MAKE

Embroider the design onto your piece of ivory silk, using the key below as a guide.

Measure and cut a piece of soft wadding to fit behind the piece.

The finished piece and the wadding must be stretched on a mat board before being mounted. Unless you are experienced at framing embroidery pieces, take the finished work to a professional framer, and select a frame and mount to suit both the piece and its eventual display position in the home.

- ivory silk
- bread dough cameo or cameo brooch
- 3m (3⅓ yds) silk ribbon, 7mm 156 (cream)
- 12m (13 yds) silk ribbon, 4mm 156 (cream)
- 6m (6½ yds) silk ribbon, 4mm 71 (pale green)
- DMC cotton: 3013 (green)
- gold metallic thread
- Mill Hill Petite Glass Beads No. 40557 (gold)
- 8 small pearls
- embroidery hoop: 22cm (8½")
- soft wadding
- pins & tape measure
- scissors
- needle & thread

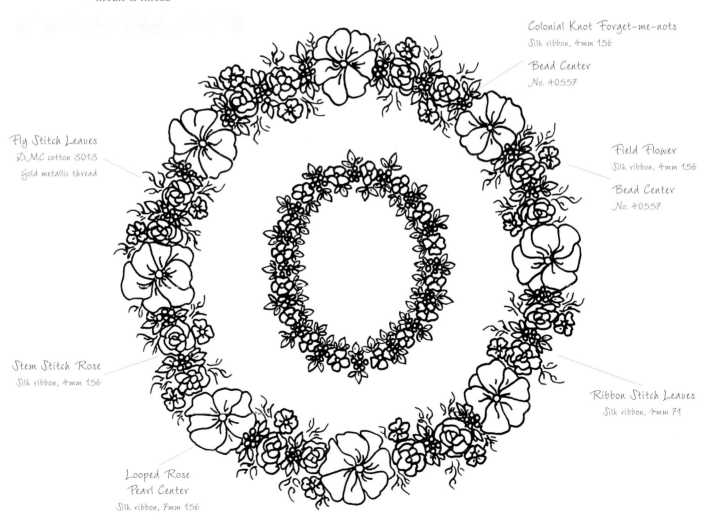

Colonial Knot Forget-me-nots
Silk ribbon, 4mm 156

Bead Center
No. 40557

Fly Stitch Leaves
DMC cotton 3013
Gold metallic thread

Field Flower
Silk ribbon, 4mm 156

Bead Center
No. 40557

Stem Stitch Rose
Silk ribbon, 4mm 156

Ribbon Stitch Leaves
Silk ribbon, 4mm 71

Looped Rose
Pearl Center
Silk ribbon, 7mm 156

Actual size

Flower Spray

TO MAKE

Embroider the flower spray design (see page 104) using the key shown below as a guide.

Using one strand of DMC cotton, embroider the bullion leaves working eight twists on one side of the leaf and ten twists on the other side of the leaf.

For the bullion flowers work six twists.

Measure and cut a piece of soft wadding to fit the piece.

The finished piece and the wadding must be stretched on a mat board before being mounted. Unless you are experienced at framing embroidery pieces, take the finished work to a professional framer, and select a frame and mount to suit both the piece and its eventual display position in the home.

The embroidery will need to be recessed in the frame.

- pure silk fabric
- 50cm (19½") Makuba rayon ribbon, No. 1505 13mm, No. 28 (burgundy)
- 20cm (7½") organdy ribbon (burgundy)
- 2m (78") silk ribbon, 4mm, 171 (dark green), 56 (green)
- 1m (39") silk ribbon, 4mm 126 (dark blue), 125 (blue), 34 (beige), 53 (yellow)
- DMC cottons: 315 (burgundy), 316 (pink), 730 (dark green), 3012 (green), 830 (brown)
- Mill Hill Petite Glass Beads No. 40557 (gold)
- embroidery hoop: 22cm (8½")
- soft wadding
- pins & tape measure
- scissors
- needle & thread

Tea Rose
Rayon ribbon 28
Organdy ribbon

Satin Stitch Leaves
Silk Ribbon 4mm 171, 56

Stem Stitch Stems
DMC cotton 830

Bullion Stitch Flower
DMC cottons 315, 316

Stem Stitch Stems
DMC cotton 3012

Bullion Stitch Leaves
DMC cottons 730, 312

Stem Stitch Stems
DMC cotton 3012

Straight Stitch Rose Bud
Rayon ribbon 28

Colonial Knot & Stem Stitch
DMC cotton 3012

Straight Stitch Calyx
Silk ribbon 4mm 171

Straight Stitch Forget-me-not
Silk ribbon 4mm, 125, 126, 34, 53

Bead Center
No. 40557

Basket of Flowers

- 1m (39") Makuba graduation ribbon, 25mm No. 4881, No. 2
- 90cm (35") Makuba luminous ribbon, 23mm No. 4599, No. 9 (old gold)
- 80cm (31") Makuba rayon, No. 1505, No. 43 (orange)
- 1.5m (1⅔ yds) Makuba rayon No. 1505, No. 14 (gold)
- 1m (39") Makuba rayon No. 1505, No. 8 (plum)
- 50cm (19½") Makuba rayon No. 1505, No. 16 (dark green)
- 1m (39") silk ribbon, 7mm No. 65 (mushroom)
- 2.5m (2⅔ yds) silk ribbon, 4mm No. 53 (yellow)
- 60cm (23½") silk ribbon, 4mm No. 164 (fawn)
- DMC cottons: 936 (dark green), 3012 (green), 372 (pale green), 3032 (grey green), 611 (khaki green), 313 (burgundy), 310 (black), 452 (pale mauve), 869 (light brown), 680 (old gold), 422 (yellow)
- gold metallic thread
- soft wadding
- pins & tape measure
- scissors
- needle & thread

TO MAKE

Trace the design shown on the opposite page.

Embroider the basket and the flowers, using the key (opposite) as a guide.

To embroider the basket handle, thread a needle with one strand of DMC cotton 869 and one of 680. Work two rows of stem stitch 5mm (¼")apart, then whip the thread over the two rows of stem stitch.

Make three ribbon roses using the graduation ribbon No. 2, three of luminous ribbon No. 9, three of rayon ribbon No. 14 and three of rayon ribbon No. 43. Stitch in place using the design as a guide. Tie a bow

onto the basket handle and stitch in place using the gold metallic thread.

Measure and cut a piece of soft wadding to fit the embroidered piece.

The finished piece and the wadding must be stretched on a mat board before being mounted. Unless you are experienced at framing embroidery pieces, take the finished work to a professional framer, and select a frame and mount to suit both the piece and its eventual display position in the home.

The finished embroidery will need to be recessed within the frame.

Increase tracing to 118%

Basket Bow
Rayon Ribbon 14
Gold Metallic Thread

Stem Stitch & Satin Stitch Basket
DMC Cotton 869. 680

Straight Stitch Black Eye Susans
Silk Ribbon, 4mm No 53

Colonial Knot Center
DMC Cotton 310

Satin Stitch Leaves
DMC cotton 3032

Stem Stitch Stems
DMC cotton 3032

Fly Stitch Leaves
DMC cotton 3032

Straight Stitch Large Wild Rose
Rayon ribbon 8

Colonial Knot Center
DMC Cotton 422

Extended Pistol Stitch Stamen
DMC cotton 310

Straight Stitch Small Wild Rose
Silk Ribbon, 7mm 65

Colonial Knot Center
DMC Cotton 422

Extended Pistol Stitch Stamen
DMC cotton 452

Ribbon Stitch Leaves
Rayon Ribbon 16

Straight Stitch
Silk Ribbon, 4mm 164

Bullion Stitch Fuschia Bud
DMC Cotton 315

Extended Pistol Stitch Stamen
DMC cotton 3032

Stem Stitch Stems & Calyx
DMC cotton 3032

Straight Stitch Black Eye Susan Buds
Silk Ribbon, 4mm No 53

Straight Stitch Calyx & Stem Stitch Stems
DMC Cotton 936

Satin Stitch Leaves
DMC Cotton 3012

49

GIFT IDEAS

*H*omemade gifts convey the thought and effort you have put into their creation and also showcase your embroidery skills. Whether for a shower tea, a wedding, a house warming, a coming-of-age birthday or for Christmas, make one of these unique and elegant gifts to show how much you care. For that extra special occasion or person you could make a set of these beautiful gifts in co-ordinating colors.

Lavender & Rose Rolls

- pins & tape measure
- scissors
- needle & thread
- sewing machine

Lavender Roll
- lavender organdie, 37cm x 13cm (14½" x 5")
- lavender ribbon, 30cm (11½")
- 1m (39") silk ribbon, 4mm, 178 (pale lavender), 179 (lavender)
- DMC cotton: 372 (green)
- gold metallic knitting yarn
- lavender pot pourri

Rose Roll
- pink organdie: 37cm x 13cm (14½" x 5")
- 1m (39") silk ribbon, 7mm, 158 (pink), 157 (pale pink)
- 50cm (19½") silk ribbon, 4mm, 171 (green), 56 (green)
- DMC cotton: 372 (green)
- gold metallic knitting yarn
- rose pot pourri

TO MAKE

Embroider the design onto the center of the fabric using the key as a guide.

With right sides facing, sew a seam along the length of the fabric. Turn right side out.

At both ends of the roll turn in a 5cm (2") seam.

Attach one end of the piece of the ribbon (use pink ribbon for the Rose Roll and lavender ribbon for the Lavender Roll) to the base of the turned-in seam.

Fill the roll with rose or lavender pot pourri up to the base of the second turned seam and attach the other end of the ribbon.

Colonial Knots & Straight Stitch Tops
DMC cotton 372

Straight Stitch Lavender
Silk ribbon, 4mm 178, 179

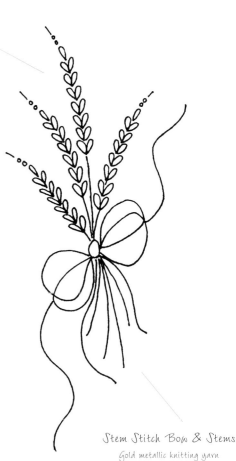

Ribbon Stitch Leaves
Silk ribbon, 4mm 171, 56

Stem Stitch Bows
Gold metallic knitting yarn

Ribbon Rose Bud
Silk ribbon, 7mm 158, 157

Ribbon Stitch Calyx
Silk ribbon, 4mm 171

Fly Stitch Leaves
DMC cotton 372

Tea Rose
Silk ribbon, 7mm 158, 157

Stem Stitch Bow & Stems
Gold metallic knitting yarn
DMC cotton 372

Actual size

Cosmetics Bag

* water-marked taffeta 30cm x 26cm (11½" x 10")
* lining fabric 30cm x 26cm (11½" x 10")
* 2.5m (100") 15mm organdy ribbon
  No. 1500, color No. 35
* 1m (39") rayon ribbon No. 1505, color No. 18
* 90cm (35") 15mm organdy ribbon
  No. 1520, color No. 49
* DMC cottons: 680 (gold), 610 (green)
* gold metallic knitting yarn
* pins & tape measure
* scissors
* needle & thread
* sewing machine

TO MAKE

Embroider, using the key as guide.

Embroider the bullion leaves using two strands of DMC cotton. Work fifteen twists on one side and twenty twists on the other side.

With right sides facing, machine stitch the fabric pieces together. Turn the bag right side out and lightly press the seams.

Stitch the lining bag in the same way as the cosmetics bag, leaving a small opening of approximately 6cm (2½") in the seam at the bottom of the lining bag.

With right sides facing, place the embroidered bag into the lining bag and stitch a seam around the top of the bags.

Pull bags right side out through the opening in the bottom of the lining bag and slip stitch the opening.

Push the lining back into the cosmetics bag. Tie the bag with a generous bow.

Extended Pistol Stitch Flower
DMC cotton 680

Bullion Stitch Leaves
DMC cotton 610

Ribbon Buds
Organdy ribbon No. 35

Ribbon Stitch Leaves
Rayon ribbon No. 18

Ribbon Roses
Organdy ribbon No. 35

Stem Stitch Bow
Gold metallic knitting yarn

Stem Stitch Stems
DMC cotton 610

Actual size

Lingerie Bag

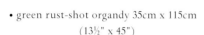

- green rust-shot organdy 35cm x 115cm (13½" x 45")
- 2m (2½yd) Makuba crepe Georgette ribbon No. 4546, 15mm, No. 66 (rust)
- 60cm (23½") Makuba crepe Georgette ribbon No. 4546, 15mm, No. 14 (old gold)
- 60cm (23½") Makuba luminous ribbon No. 4549, 13mm, No. 10 (brown)
- 50cm (19½") Makuba luminous ribbon No. 4599, 13mm, No. 5 (green)
- 130cm (51") Makuba organdy ribbon No. 4563, 75mm, No. 13 (green) for the bow
- DMC cottons: 377 (rust), 732 (green)
- pins & tape measure
- scissors
- sewing machine

TO MAKE

Fold the fabric in half lengthwise.

Work four tea roses, positioning them on the front of the bag using the key and design shown below as a guide.

Make three luminous ribbon roses, three crepe georgette ribbon roses and twelve luminous ribbon leaves and sew them in place around the center tea roses.

Embroider the bullion rose buds using two strands of DMC cotton. Work fifteen twists on one side of the bud and twenty twists on the other. Work fifteen twists for the calyx.

With right sides facing, sew up the side seams. Neaten and turn right side out.

Turn over a 1cm (¼") seam, press and then turn over a 10cm (3½") seam and press again.

Using one strand of DMC cotton stem stitch around the bottom and top of the turned seam. Tie the top of the bag with a generous bow.

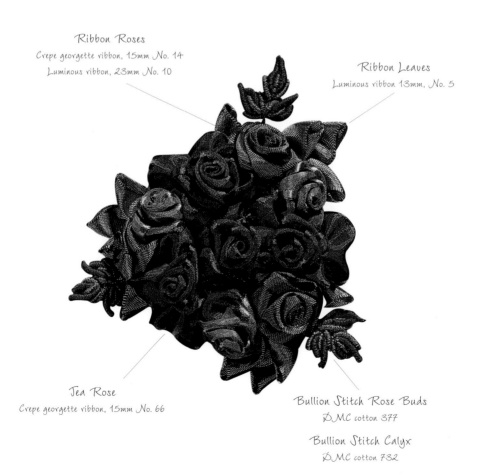

Ribbon Roses
Crepe georgette ribbon, 15mm No. 14
Luminous ribbon, 23mm No. 10

Ribbon Leaves
Luminous ribbon 13mm, No. 5

Tea Rose
Crepe georgette ribbon, 15mm No. 66

Bullion Stitch Rose Buds
DMC cotton 377

Bullion Stitch Calyx
DMC cotton 732

Jewelry Cushion

- burgundy fabric
- 70cm (27½") burgundy tassel braid
- polyester filling
- 1.5m (1⅓ yds) Makuba rayon ribbon, 13mm No. 1505, No. 28 (burgundy)
- 1m (39") Pan Pacific organdy ribbon, 24mm No. 1083, No. 8 (burgundy)
- 60cm (23½") Makuba luminous ribbon, 13mm No. 4599, No. 9 (green)
- pins & tape measure
- scissors
- needle & thread
- sewing machine

TO MAKE

Make three large ribbon roses by placing the rayon ribbon on top of the organdy ribbon and fold them together.

Make five small rayon ribbon roses and five small organdie ribbon roses.

Make nine small rayon ribbon rose buds and fourteen luminous ribbon leaves.

Sew the roses, buds and leaves onto the cushion front using the design and key shown below as a guide.

Pin the template onto the fabric, making sure that the roses are centralized within the square, and cut out.

Cut a second square of fabric.

With right sides facing, tack the fabric squares together.

Machine stitch the seams of the cushion leaving an opening of approximately 6cm (2½").

Turn the cushion right side out and press lightly around all of the seams.

Pack the cushion evenly with polyester filling to gain the desired thickness and then slip stitch the opening closed.

Hand stitch the tassel braid around the edge of the cushion.

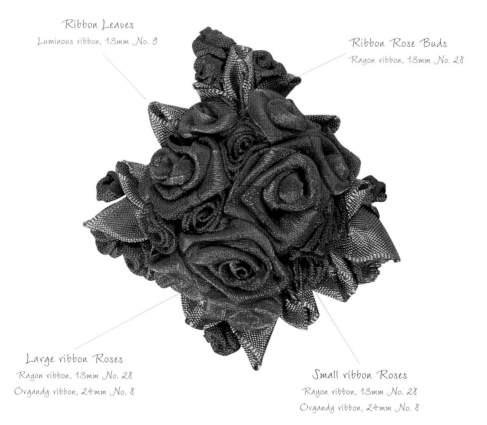

Ribbon Leaves
Luminous ribbon, 13mm No. 9

Ribbon Rose Buds
Rayon ribbon, 13mm No. 28

Large ribbon Roses
Rayon ribbon, 13mm No. 28
Organdy ribbon, 24mm No. 8

Small ribbon Roses
Rayon ribbon, 13mm No. 28
Organdy ribbon, 24mm No. 8

Circular Basket

- small circular basket
- gold satin
- 40cm (15½") silk ribbon, 7mm, 135 (soft peach)
- 1m (39") silk ribbon, 7mm, 156 (cream)
- 1m (39") silk ribbon, 4mm, 90 (pale blue), 125 (blue), 31 (pale green), 32 (green)
- DMC cotton: 502 (green)
- Rajmahal No. 45 (gold)
- Mill Hill Petite Glass Beads No. 40557 (gold)
- embroidery hoop: 11.5cm (4½")

TO MAKE

Embroider the design onto the gold satin using the key (shown below) as a guide.

Cut out the embroidered fabric allowing enough to turn in a small hem. Depending on the type of basket you have chosen, either slip stitch, tack, or glue the embroidered piece to the top of the basket.

TO FINISH

Using a complementary color thread, stem stitch one or two rows around the edge of the basket.

Stem Stitch Lattice
Rajmahal No. 45

Bead Center
No. 40557

Colonial Knot
Forget-me-not
Silk ribbon, 4mm 90, 125

Bead Center
No. 40557

Ribbon Stitch Leaves
Silk ribbon, 4mm 31, 32

Stem Stitch Stems
DMC cotton 502

Tea Rose
Silk ribbon, 7mm 135, 156

Actual size

Oval Basket

• small oval basket
• silk fabric
• 2m (2½ yds) silk ribbon, 4mm,
135 (soft peach), 156 (cream)
• 2m (2½ yds) silk ribbon, 2mm 125 (blue)
• 1m (39") silk ribbon, 2mm,
31 (pale green), 32 (green)
• DMC cottons: 676 (yellow), 948 (soft peach)
• embroidery hoop: 11.5cm (4½")

TO MAKE

Embroider using the key as a guide.

Cut out the embroidered fabric allowing enough to turn in a small hem. Depending on the type of basket you have chosen, either slip stitch, tack, or glue the embroidered piece to the top of the basket.

TO FINISH

Using a complementary color thread, stem stitch one or two rows around the edge of the basket.

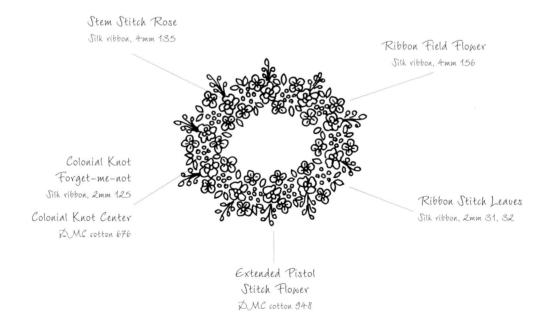

Stem Stitch Rose
Silk ribbon, 4mm 135

Ribbon Field Flower
Silk ribbon, 4mm 156

Colonial Knot
Forget-me-not
Silk ribbon, 2mm 125

Colonial Knot Center
DMC cotton 676

Ribbon Stitch Leaves
Silk ribbon, 2mm 31, 32

Extended Pistol
Stitch Flower
DMC cotton 948

Actual size

Chocolate Bear

- blanketing
- polyester filling
- 4 wooden buttons
- 2 small teddy's eyes
- lace
- small pearls
- 4m (4½ yards), silk ribbon, 7mm 135 (pale apricot)
- 1m (39") silk ribbon, 4mm 56 (green)
- DMC cottons: 3774 (apricot), 372 (green), black
- pins & tape measure
- scissors
- needle & thread
- sewing machine

Fly Stitch Leaves
DMC cotton 372

Ribbon Stitch Leaves
Silk ribbon, 4mm, No. 56

Small Pearl — Base of Leaves

Actual size

Ribbon Rose
Silk ribbon, 7mm, No. 135

Tied Bows & Straight Stitch Tails
Silk ribbon, 7mm, No. 135

TO MAKE

All 6mm (¼") seam allowances are included in the pattern. Cut out the pattern pieces on page 105.

With right sides facing, join the head side pieces together along the center front seam from the nose to the head opening. Finger press open.

With right sides facing, pin and tack the center head piece to the sides. Machine stitch in place and turn right side out. Insert the teddy's eyes.

Using a strong thread, work a running stitch around the neck opening 6mm (¼") in from the edge. Fill the head firmly with polyester filling, pull up the running stitches to gather the neck and finish off.

Place two ear pieces together, right sides facing, and stitch. Repeat for the second ear. Turn right side out and fill with polyester filling. Fold in the raw edges and slip stitch the opening of both ears. Sew the ears in place on the head.

Sew a satin stitch nose and a stem stitch mouth in black DMC cotton to complete the teddy's head.

With right sides facing, stitch arm pieces together, leaving a small opening on the side. Turn right side out and fill with polyester filling. Slip stitch the opening closed.

With right sides facing, stitch front and back seams of the leg pieces, leaving a small side opening. Stitch the soles to the legs. Turn right side out, fill with polyester filling and slip stitch openings closed.

With right sides facing, stitch around the body, leaving an opening on the back. Turn right side out.

Attach the arms and legs to the teddy's body using the wooden buttons.

Firmly pack the body with polyester filling and slip stitch the back opening closed.

Slip stitch the head to the body.

Sew ribbon roses onto the teddy's head and tummy and embroider using the design and key as a guide.

TO FINISH

Gather a piece of lace to make a collar.

65

Wild Pansy
Bed Jacket

- blanketing 95cm (37½") square, (silver grey)
- lace collar
- 6m (20') silk ribbon, 7mm 84 (deep purple)
- 1m (39") silk ribbon, 4mm,
  53 (yellow), 13 (pale yellow)
- 3m (10') silk ribbon, 4mm 171 (dark green)
- DMC Broder Medicis: 8508 (grey)
- DMC cottons: 327 (deep purple), 936 (dark green)
- fabric pen
- scissors
- needle & thread

TO MAKE

For the patterns, scallop templates and placement guide refer to pages 106 and 107.

Using a fabric pen trace around the scallop templates.

Cut out the scalloped edge, up the front opening and around the jacket neckline.

Buttonhole stitch the scallops, front opening and the neckline using one strand of DMC Medicis 8508.

Hand stitch the lace collar to the neckline.

Using two strands of DMC cotton 327 work colonial knots around the scalloped edge of the jacket.

Embroider the design using the key (shown below) as a guide.

Straight Stitch Bud
Silk ribbon, 7mm 84

Straight Stitch Calyx
Silk ribbon, 4mm 171

Stem Stitch Stems
DMC cotton 936

Straight Stitch Petals
Silk ribbon, 7mm 84

Straight Stitch Center Petals
Silk ribbon, 4mm 13, 53

Straight Stitch Calyx
Silk ribbon, 4mm 171

Straight Stitch Center
DMC cotton 327

Stem Stitch Stems
DMC cotton 936

Satin Stitch Leaves
Silk ribbon, 4mm 171

Stem Stitch Stems
DMC cotton 936

Bow
Silk ribbon, 7mm 84

Colonial Knot Anchor
DMC cotton 327

Wild Pansy
Slippers

- soft leather
- blanketing
- lining fabric
- iron-on interfacing
- quick-drying craft glue
- 1.25m (49") satin binding (pale yellow)
- 1.50m (59") silk ribbon, 7mm 84 (deep purple)
- 90cm (35") silk ribbon, 4mm,
  53 (yellow), 13 (pale yellow)
- 1.20m (47") silk ribbon, 4mm 171 (green)
- DMC cottons: 327 (deep purple), 936 (dark green)
- DMC Broder Medicis: 8508 (grey)
- fabric marking pen
- pins & tape measure
- scissors
- needle & thread
- sewing machine
- iron

TO MAKE

All 6mm (¼") seam allowances are included in the pattern. The pattern provided for the slippers is an adult medium size. For other sizes cut a sole to fit the foot and shorten or lengthen the back seams of the pattern piece provided.

Cut two shoe soles of leather and two of lining using the slippers pattern, (see page 108). Cut two shoe uppers of blanketing, two of lining and two of iron-on interfacing. Cut two shoe fronts and two of lining in blanketing.

Transfer the slippers design, (page 69), onto the slipper front. Embroider the slipper front following the key as a guide.

Tack the blanket lining to the embroidered slipper front. Using Medicis 8058, buttonhole stitch around the scalloped edge.

Work the colonial knots in two strands of DMC cotton 327 as shown on the slipper front pattern.

Apply a thin layer of glue around the edge of the leather soles, shiny side up, and stick the fabric lining to the soles, right sides facing up. Iron the iron-on interfacing onto the back of the fabric lining.

Stitch a 5mm (¼") back seam on the lining and blanket uppers. Press seams flat. Tack the top of the lining and blanket uppers together, right sides facing in and sew a 5mm (¼") seam.

Turn right side out, press and tack the lining and blanket together around the bottom of the uppers.

Position the embroidered front onto the shoe upper. Using the Medicis wool, stitch in place along the scalloped edge. With the right sides facing up, sew the uppers to the soles.

Machine sew the satin binding around the edge of the leather sole placing the join at the center back. Fold binding over and hand stitch in place on the blanket uppers.

TO FINISH

Using two strands of DMC cotton 327, stem stitch around the edge of the satin binding and the top of the uppers.

Attach an outer sole on the slipper by placing the slipper onto a piece of leather, shiny side up. Trace around the sole of the slipper and cut out.

Spread a thin layer of glue over the slipper sole and a thin layer of glue on the shiny side of the outer sole. Carefully place soles together and press firmly.

Wild Pansy
*B*rooch

TO MAKE

Construct a paper circle template with a diameter of 6cm (2½"). Using the circle template draw two circles with a fabric marking pen onto the piece of silk fabric.

Embroider a wild pansy onto one of the silk fabric circles, using the key for the slippers below.

Using the gold metallic yarn, work a chain stitch around both circles 5mm (¼") in from the circle edge and cut the circles out.

Thread a needle with six strands of DMC cotton and join the two circles together, using the chain stitch braid method on page 86 of the Stitch Glossary.

Before closing the circle completely, insert a small amount of polyester filling to slightly pad the brooch.

- gold silk
- 50cm (19½") silk ribbon, 7mm No. 84 (deep purple)
- 20cm (8") silk ribbon, 4mm No. 53 (yellow)
- 70cm (27½") silk ribbon, 4mm No. 171 (green)
- DMC cottons: 327 (deep purple), 936 (dark green)
- gold metallic knitting yarn
- polyester filling
- fabric marking pen
- pins & tape measure
- scissors
- needle & thread

Slippers design
Actual size

Left shoe

Straight Stitch Bud
Silk ribbon, 7mm 84

Straight Stitch Calyx
Silk ribbon, 4mm 171

Stem Stitch Stems
DMC cotton 936

Satin Stitch Leaves
Silk ribbon, 4mm 171

Stem Stitch Stems
DMC cotton 936

Right shoe

Straight Stitch Petals
Silk ribbon, 7mm 84

Straight Stitch Center Petals
Silk ribbon, 4mm 13, 53

Straight Stitch Calyx
Silk ribbon, 4mm 171

Straight Stitch Center
DMC cotton 327

Stem Stitch Stems
DMC cotton 936

Brooch design
Actual size

BLANKETS

*Make a blanket for every occasion! From the
cosy knee rug to the charming bluebird rug
for babies, blankets provide an opportunity for your
needlework pieces to be particularly useful and picturesquely
on display. Choose, from this range of timelessly appealing rugs,
the ones that will especially warm the hearts (and toes)
of your family and friends.*

Heritage Rose Blanket

- single bed Onkaparinga blanket (heritage green)
- Birch Tear Away for Embroidery & Applique,
  90cm x 60cm (36" x 24")
- DMC Broder Medicis: 8223 (dark pink),
  8224 (pink), 8225 (pale pink), 8211 (grey blue),
  8314 (yellow), 8426 (green), 8407 (dark green)
- sharp lead pencil
- pins & tape measure
- scissors or tweezers
- needle & thread

TO MAKE

The center panel of the blanket consists of six embroidered posies and six embroidered sprays.

Trace the embroidery designs (see page 109) around the inside edge of the 90cm x 60cm (36" x 24") piece of Tear Away. Trace a posy at each of the four corners and in the centers of the longer sides. Trace six rose sprays between the rose posies.

Position the Tear Away onto the center of the blanket and tack firmly in place. Cut away the center of the Tear Away.

Satin stitch the design working through both Tear Away and the blanket. Be sure to cover all of the traced design with your satin stitches.

When the embroidery is complete unpick the tacking and pull away the Tear Away. Remove any remaining bits and pieces with the blunt edge of a pair of scissors or tweezers.

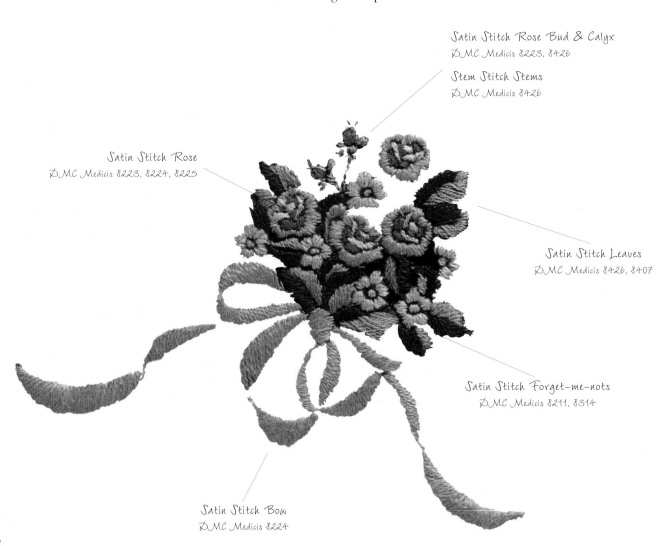

Satin Stitch Rose Bud & Calyx
DMC Medicis 8223, 8426

Stem Stitch Stems
DMC Medicis 8426

Satin Stitch Rose
DMC Medicis 8223, 8224, 8225

Satin Stitch Leaves
DMC Medicis 8426, 8407

Satin Stitch Forget-me-nots
DMC Medicis 8211, 8314

Satin Stitch Bow
DMC Medicis 8224

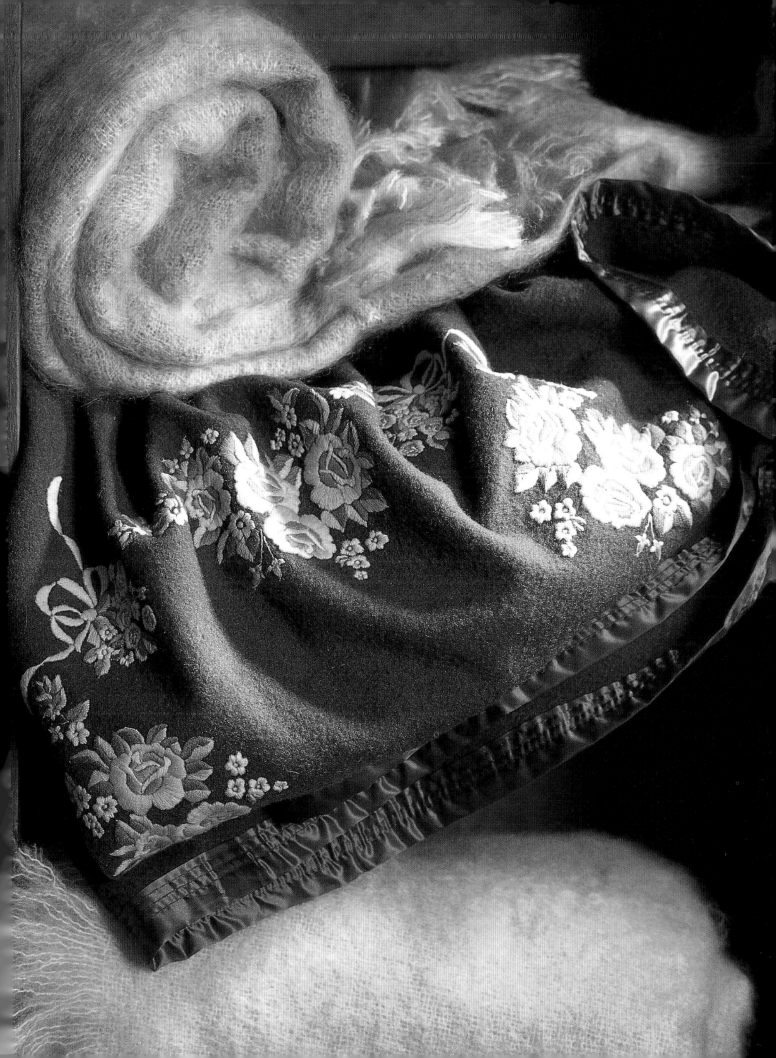

Victorian Posy Rug

- wool blanket piece (burgundy),
  94cm x 76cm (37" x 30")
- 3.5m (4 yds) beading lace
- 3.8m (4¼ yds) cotton lace, 5cm (2")
- 4m (4½ yds) silk ribbon, 7mm (black)
- DMC Broder Medicis: 8223 (dark pink),
  8224 (pink), 8225 (pale pink), 8407 (dark green),
  8405 (green), 8305 (mustard), noir
- Rajmahal 45 (gold)
- sharp lead pencil
- drawing compass
- paper
- pins & tape measure
- scissors
- needle & thread
- sewing machine

Satin Stitch Rose
DMC Medicis 8223, 8224, 8225

Satin Stitch Calyx
DMC Medicis 8405 Rajmahal 45

Colonial Knot Flower
DMC Medicis 8305

Stem Stitch Stems
DMC Medicis 8407

Satin Stitch Leaves
DMC Medicis 8405

Stem Stitch Stems
DMC Medicis 8407

Satin Stitch Rose Bud
DMC Medicis 8223

Satin Stitch Calyx
DMC Medicis 8407, 8405
Rajmahal 45

Stem Stitch Stems
DMC Medicis 8405

Satin Stitch Bow
DMC Medicis noir

TO MAKE

Construct a paper circle template with a diameter of
26cm (10"). To obtain four evenly spaced points on
the circumference of the circle, fold the template in
half and then fold into quarters.

Place a posy design (see page 110) on each quadrant
of the circle. Refer to Transferring Designs on page 84.

Embroider using the key (shown above) as a guide.

TO FINISH

To prepare the blanket for attaching the lace edging,
use one of the following three methods:
(a) overlock the edge of the blanket;
(b) sew with the sewing machine set on the widest
    zigzag stitch, e.g. use the maximum stitch length
    and width available;

(c) blanket stitch by hand.

Attach the lace, starting at the top left-hand
corner of the blanket, and allow 5cm (2") of lace to
overlap the corner.

Slightly gather the lace as you slip stitch it to the
blanket. Stop gathering the lace when you have
stitched to 4cm (1½") from the corner.

Work all four sides of the blanket, ensuring that
you gather the lace 4cm (1½") either side of corners.

When all four sides of the blanket are completed,
turn the overlapping lace under on a 45° angle. Tack
into place, cut off excess lace and overstitch by hand.

Slip stitch the beading lace onto the blanket.
Thread the ribbon through and tie a bow at the
bottom right-hand corner.

The Three Bears

- 2 pieces flannel blanketing (cream): 100cm x 75cm (39" x 29½")
- 4m (4⅓ yds) blanket binding (burgundy)
- 4m (4⅓ yds) cotton lace, 2cm (¾")
- brown blanketing
- 2 small pieces of old lace
- striped silk
- 3 x 6mm diameter round pearl shell buttons
- 2 pairs of very small teddy bear eyes
- polyester filling
- 20cm (8") silk ribbon, 4mm 4 (black)
- 70cm (27½") silk ribbon, 4mm, 171 (green), 56 (green)
- 1m (39") silk ribbon, 13mm 129 (burgundy)
- 80cm (31½") silk ribbon, 13mm 128 (rich pink)
- DMC Broder Medicis: 8816 (pink), 8818 (pink), 8412 (green), 8405 (green), 8314 (yellow), noir (black), 8839 (brown)
- Appleton's Crewel wool: 756 (bright pink)
- DMC cottons: 840 (brown), 936 (green), 315 (burgundy), black
- Rajmahal: No. 45 (gold)
- fabric marking pen
- pins & tape measure
- scissors
- needle & thread

TO MAKE

To transfer the embroidery design onto the blanket, refer to Transferring Designs on page 84. Embroider the design (see pages 110 and 111) using the key as a guide.

Using a fabric marking pen, trace the bear patterns onto the piece of brown blanketing and cut out. Cut two pattern pieces for baby bear and two arm pattern pieces for mother bear.

Stitch the baby's eyes, nose and mouth using one strand of DMC cotton (black).

Using one strand of DMC cotton 840, buttonhole stitch the baby bear pieces together and pack with a small amount of polyester filling before closing.

Stem stitch the ears, face, arms, hands, legs and body outlines, using the same thread as above.

Make a collar using a small piece of lace and attach it to baby bear's neck. At the collar top, sew three colonial knot roses using two strands of DMC cotton 315 and three daisy stitch leaves 936.

Buttonhole stitch mother bear's arm pieces together and lightly pack with polyester filling before closing. Insert the eyes and stitch in the noses and mouths of the parent bears.

Position the bears on the blanket and tack in place.

Using one strand of DMC cotton 840, buttonhole stitch the bears to the blanket and lightly pack with polyester filling before

Colonial Knot Flower
Appleton's 756

Stem Stitch Stems
DMC Medicis 8405

Satin Stitch Leaves
DMC Medicis 8405

Stem Stitch Stems
DMC Medicis 8412

Satin Stitch Flower
DMC Medicis 8314

Colonial Knot Center
DMC Medicis Black

Stem Stitch Stems
DMC Medicis 8839

Satin Stitch Center Petals
DMC Medicis 8816, Appleton's 756

Button Hole Stitch
Outside Petals
DMC Medicis 8818

Satin Stitch Calyx
DMC Medicis 8412
Rajmahal 45

Button Hole Stitch Leaves
DMC Medicis 8405, 8412

Stem Stitch Stems
DMC Medicis 8839

Satin Stitch Bow
Appleton's 756

Stem Stitch Outline
Rajmahal 45

closing. Stem stitch the ears, face, arms, hands, legs and body outlines.

Sew a lace collar around mother bear's neck. Attach her arm using one of the small buttons. Sew a button on her leg and one on father bear's arm. Cut out father bear's vest, turn a small seam and slip stitch onto his body. Tie a bow tie from silk ribbon.

Make up four ribbon roses using silk ribbon 128 and five using 129. Use five roses, three of pink and two of burgundy, for mother bear's head wreath and one of burgundy for her collar.

Embroider ribbon stitch leaves using silk ribbon 171 and 56 amongst the wreath roses. Stem stitch wreath bow using Appleton's wool 756 and one strand of Rajmahal No. 45. Stitch three ribbon roses, two of burgundy and one of pink, in place for father bear's posy. Embroider ribbon stitch leaves using silk ribbon 171 and 56 around the posy. Work a stem stitch in one strand of DMC cotton 936 for the posy stems.

Place the completed baby bear in mother bear's arms and stitch it in place.

Tack the blanket and the blanket lining together.

Refer to the instructions given on page 95 for details on how to create a satin binding finish. Using six strands of Rajmahal No. 45, stem stitch around the edge of the lace.

The Tired Twins

- flannel blanketing (cream):
  100cm x 75cm (39" x 29½")
- cotton waffle blanketing (cream):
  100cm x 75cm (39" x 29½") for lining
- 4m (4⅓ yds) blanket binding (white)
- brown blanketing
- 4 x 6mm diameter round pearl shell buttons
- polyester filling
- 1.5m (59") silk ribbon, 7mm 157 (pink)
- 50cm (19½") silk ribbon, 4mm,
  171 (dark green),56 (green)
- DMC Broder Medicis: 8224 (pink),
  8225 (pink), 8328 (yellow), 8421 (green),
  8420 (green), 8211 (blue), Ecru
- DMC cottons: 840 (brown), 310 (black)
- Rajmahal No. 45 (gold)
- fabric marking pen
- needle & thread
- scissors

TO MAKE

To transfer the embroidery design (see page 112) onto the blanket refer to Transferring Designs on page 84.

The bullion roses consist of six twists for the rose center, ten twists for the inner petals and fifteen twists for the outside petals.

Embroider the bullion leaves working eight twists on one side of the leaf and ten twists on the other.

Using a fabric marking pen, trace the bear patterns onto the piece of brown blanketing and cut out.

Satin stitch the bears' eyes and nose, using one strand of DMC cotton 310 (black).

Position the bears onto the blanket and tack in place.

Using one strand of DMC cotton 840 (brown), buttonhole stitch the bears to the blanket and lightly pack with polyester filling before closing.

Stem stitch the ears, face, arms, legs and body outlines.

Make up eight ribbon roses using silk ribbon, 7mm (157) and attach around the neck of the bears.

Surround the roses with ribbon stitch leaves.

Sew the arm and leg buttons in place.

TO FINISH

Tack the blanket piece and lining together.

Refer to the instructions given on page 95 for details on how to create a satin binding finish. Using one strand of Broder Medicis 8225, stem stitch around the edge of the binding.

Satin Stitch Flower
DMC Medicis 8211

Colonial Knot Center
DMC Medicis 8328

Bullion Stitch Leaves
DMC Medicis 8421, 8420

Stem Stitch Stems
DMC Medicis 8421

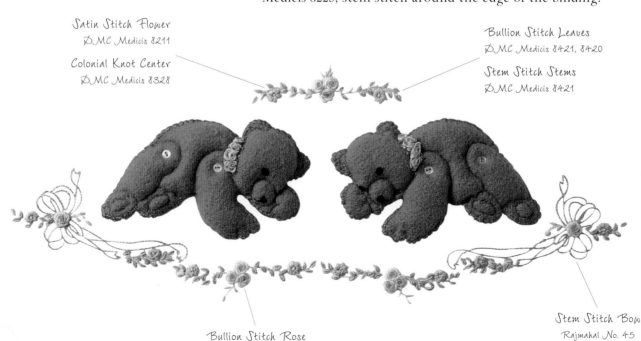

Bullion Stitch Rose
DMC Medicis 8224, 8225, Ecru

Stem Stitch Bow
Rajmahal No. 45

Bluebird Baby's Blanket

• flannel blanketing (cream):
100cm x 75cm (39" x 29½")
• 4m (4½ yds) blanket binding (blue)
• 4m (4½ yds) cotton lace, width 1.5cm (½")
• DMC Broder Medicis: 8405 (green), 8314 (yellow),
8211 (blue), 8224 (pink), 8225 (pale pink), 8119
(dusky pink), 8839 (brown), 8314 (yellow)
• sharp lead pencil
• drawing compass
• paper
• fabric marking pen
• pins & tape measure
• scissors
• needle & thread
• sewing machine

TO MAKE

Construct a circle template out of paper with a diameter of 35cm
(13½"). Fold the circle template into eight equal sections.

Pin the circle template onto the center of the blanket and tack
around it with cotton thread.

Using a fabric marking pen mark the positions of the eight
sections on the circumference of the circle.

To transfer the design onto the blanket refer to Transferring
Designs on page 84.

Embroider the design using the key (shown below) as a guide.
The bullion roses consist of ten twists for the center bullion.
Twelve twists are worked on either side.

TO FINISH

Refer to the instructions given on page 95 for details on how to
create a satin binding finish. Using the DMC Broder Medicis 8211
(blue), stem stitch around the edge of the lace.

Stem Stitch Bird
Colonial Knot Eye
Satin Stitch Beak
DMC Medicis 8211, 8839, 8314

Bullion Stitch Rose
DMC Medicis 8224, 8225

Stem Stitch Bow
DMC Medicis 8119

Colonial Knot
Forget-me-not
DMC Medicis 8211, 8314

Daisy Stitch Leaves
DMC Medicis 8405

Actual size

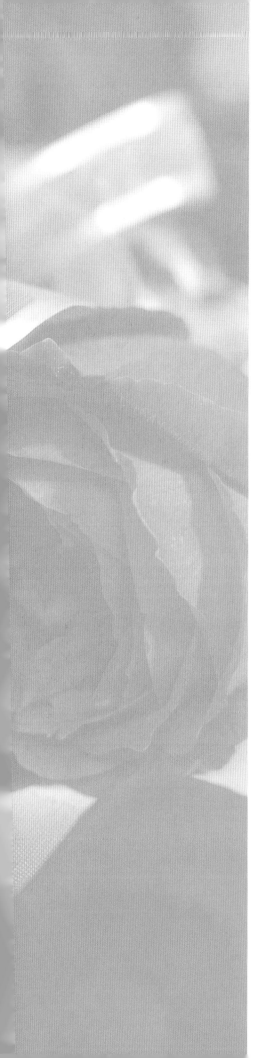

GENERAL INFORMATION

here are so many facets to skilled needlework that it can be difficult to keep them all fresh in your mind. Here are a few how-to reminders and hints to help you on the path to enjoyable and successful creation with ribbons and roses. All the materials, patterns, stitches, and information you need to begin and complete the projects shown in this book are set out here for you to refer to when you need them. Where possible, lists are in alphabetical order, to make it easier for you to locate what you need.

MATERIALS

These materials were used to create the projects shown in this book.

Accessories

• Mill Hill Glass Beads.
• But Baby Buttons 6mm diameter, Round Pearl Shell Button, available from Stadia Handcrafts, NSW.
• Hand painted roses on silk fabric, available from Lee Lockheed Designs.

Cottons and Threads

• DMC Broder Medicis: (Art No. 475), 2 ply crewel wool.
• DMC Stranded Cotton (Art No. 117), 100% cotton lustrous thread in six separable strands.
• Marlitt, a polyester thread with a shiny finish, in four separable strands.
• Rajmahal (Art silk/viscose), a thread with a shiny finish in six separable strands.
• Gold metallic thread.
• Metallic knitting yarn.
Available through most specialist embroidery outlets.

Embroidery Hoops

• Embroidery flexi hoops sizes 11.5cm (4½") and 22cm (8½") were used for the ribbon projects featured in this book.

Fabrics

With an exquisite range of fabrics to choose from, spend some time searching through the remnant box of your favorite fabric stores. You will be surprised at what you will find.

The fabrics I have chosen for the projects in the book are: 100% wool blanketing, wool flannel blanketing, raw silk, fine silk, silk satin-backed crepe, organza and upholstery fabrics.

Needles

Because needles vary in thickness, length, size of eye and sharpness of point, I prefer to use Birch needles. I find these needles have an excellent range of eyelet sizes that cater for all of my embroidery needs. Select the appropriate needles for your embroidery from the list following.

For embroidery with	use these needles
DMC Broder Medicis	Birch Embroidery Crewel, size 3/9 or 5/10
DMC Stranded Cotton	Birch Embroidery Crewel, size 3/9 or 5/10
Marlitt	Birch Embroidery Crewel, size 3/9 or 5/10
Rajmahal	Birch Embroidery Crewel, size 3/9 or 5/10
Metallic thread	Birch Embroidery Crewel, size 3/9 or 5/10
Knitting yarn	Birch Tapestry, size 20
Silk ribbon, 2mm and 4mm	Birch Chenille or Tapestry, size 24–26
Silk ribbon, 7mm	Birch Chenille or Tapestry, size 22

Pens

• Hot Iron Transfer Pencil (see Transferring Designs).
• Birch Marking Pen with Eraser—purple water-soluble ink on one end and white eraser ink on the other end. This pen is excellent for drawing patterns or marking designs on all types of fabrics.

Ribbons and Laces

• Cotton On Creations (NSW): silk ribbon, 100% silk, organdy ribbon and lace.
• Pan Pacific Distributing Co. (NSW): organdy ribbon.
• Designer Trim (Vic): Makuba ribbon.
These are all available through most specialist embroidery outlets.

Scissors

The serious embroiderer should invest in a pair of high quality embroidery scissors. The scissors should be small with sharp, perfectly closing, pointed blades.

TRANSFERRING DESIGNS

Many of the projects require a design transfer. Here are some handy hints on successful transfers.

Hot Iron Transfer Pencil

A good quality transfer pencil can be used successfully on fabrics such as linens, cottons, calico and silk. Draw the pattern on heavy-duty tracing paper, turn the paper over and trace over the lines with the transfer pencil. Place the design (transfer pencil side down) onto the fabric. Hold a hot iron over the transfer for a few seconds. Carefully lift a corner of paper to make sure that the design is transferring. The Three Bears Blanket and The Bluebird Baby's Blanket designs on pages 76 and 80 respectively can be transferred in this manner. Extreme care must be taken not to scorch the fine flannel wool blanketing.

Transferring Designs onto Wool

Trace the design onto good quality tracing paper. Tack or pin the design onto the woollen blanketing and, with a sharp lead pencil or water-soluble fabric marking pen, pierce a hole through the center of each flower on the tracing paper, making sure to mark a small dot on the fabric. When you remove the tracing paper you are left with the dots that mark the center of each flower, on which you can now work the design. Break larger designs into smaller, more workable sections.

I discovered that if I ironed the pile of thick woollen blanketing perfectly flat I could use the hot iron-on transfer method. I found this method to be very successful for the satin stitch designs and used it for the Victorian Posy Rug on page 74. Once the blanket was embroidered the pile of the blanket quickly returned to its natural state. I would not, however, recommend this method for large designs. For the larger satin stitch designs use Birch Tear Away for Embroidery and Applique.

Transferring Bows

To transfer a bow, cut out a template of paper and tack it to the fabric. Using the same color thread as the bow, outline the shape using a small running stitch. Unpick the tacking on the template and remove it. Satin stitch the bow, working either side of the running stitches. As an alternative to the hot iron-on transfer method, the bluebirds on page 80 can be transferred in this manner, working a stem stitch over the running stitches.

TASSEL MAKING

Materials Needed

- cardboard: 7cm x 5cm (2¾" x 2")
- DMC cotton: (ecru)
- Marlitt 1034 (ivory)
- Mill Hill Petite Glass Beads No. 40123
- pins & tape measure
- scissors
- needle & thread

To Make

Wrap the Marlitt and DMC embroidery cottons in approximately equal proportions around the cardboard to desired thickness.

Insert a hanging thread under the wrapped thread at the top of the cardboard.

Carefully slide the wound thread off the cardboard.

Using a length of thread, hold the tail in place with your thumb and finger, and tightly wrap the skein approximately 1.3cm (½") down from the center fold.

Finish wrapping by tucking the tail end of the thread under the wrapped section.

Sew Petite Beads around the wrapped section.

Cut the bottom loops of the tassel.

Use the hanging thread to attach the tassel to the center of the cushion (or to the center of the baby's coat hanger).

STITCH GLOSSARY

This section describes the various embroidery stitches and silk ribbon stitches used throughout the book.

EMBROIDERY STITCHES

Bullion Stitch

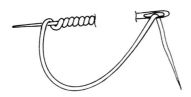

Pick up a back stitch the size of the bullion stitch required. Bring the needlepoint out where it first emerged but do not pull the needle through. Twist the thread as many times as is required to equal the space of the back stitch. Hold the coils with your thumb and finger and ease the thread through. Insert the needle back to your starting point to anchor the bullion knot.

Buttonhole Stitch

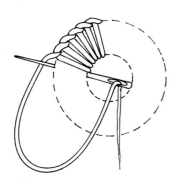

Bring the thread out on the lower (inner) line. Insert the needle on the upper (outer) line (diagram 1), taking a straight downward stitch with the thread below the needle. Pull the stitch up to form a loop and repeat the stitch working around the circle.

Chain Stitch

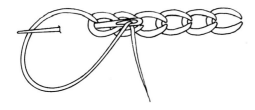

Bring the thread through the fabric. Hold the thread to the left with the thumb of the left hand. Insert the needle where it last emerged and bring the needle point out again a short distance away. Loop the thread around the needle towards you. Pull through. Repeat the loop by inserting the needle point back to exactly where the thread came out in the previous loop.

Chain Stitch Braid

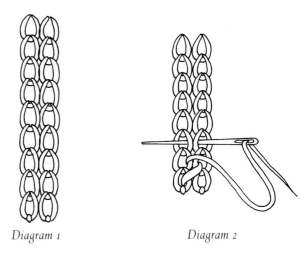

Diagram 1   *Diagram 2*

Work two parallel rows of chain stitch (diagram 1). Bring the needle up through the fabric into the center of the first chain stitch on the left-hand side. Pass the needle from right to left through the two chain stitches immediately above, passing over the outer stitches and under the inner stitches (diagram 2). Continue in this manner until the braid is complete.

Colonial Knot

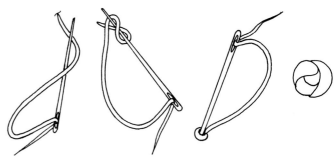

Bring the needle up through the fabric. Hold the thread taut with the left hand away from the fabric. Place the needle under the thread to the right and lift the thread up over the needle from left to right creating a figure eight. Insert the needle into the fabric close to where it emerged and pull the working thread taut with your left hand so that a firm and tight knot is formed.

Daisy Stitch

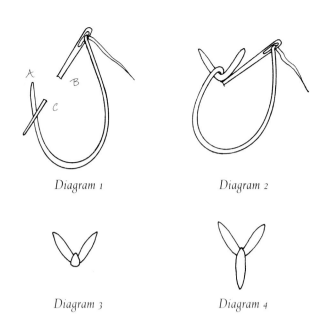

Diagram 1   *Diagram 2*

Diagram 3   *Diagram 4*

When commencing the daisy, work from the inside to the outer edge. Bring the needle and thread through the fabric at the base of the petal. Insert the needle back where it first emerged and bring it up again just inside the tip of the petal. Loop the thread around the needle and pull the thread through. Anchor it at the top of the petal with a small stitch. Bring the needle up through the back of your work to start the next petal.

Extended Pistol Stitch

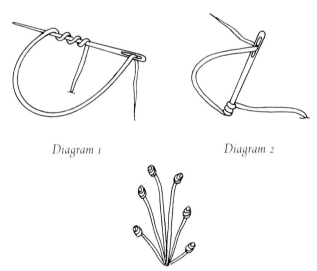

Diagram 1   *Diagram 2*

Bring the needle through the fabric. Hold the thread taut and place the needle across the thread away from the exit point. Wrap the thread around the needle four or five times (diagram 1). Keep the stalk taut and re-insert the needle into the fabric for the length of the required stitch (diagram 2).

Fly Stitch

Fly stitch is great for forming leaves and also for connecting flowers, such as forget-me-nots and rose buds. Bring the needle out through to the left of where the stitch is required (point A). Take the needle across a little to the right (point B) and take a

small stitch downwards to the center (point C). With the thread below the needle, pull the thread through and insert the needle again below the stitch at the center and anchor in place (diagram 2).

Fly Stitch Leaves

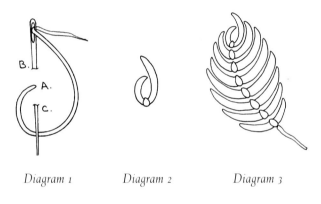

Diagram 1   *Diagram 2*   *Diagram 3*

To form the fly stitch leaf, bring the needle up through the fabric at point A (diagram 1). Insert the needle tip at point B directly above point A and return the needle tip back to point C, directly below point A. Keeping the thread below the needle, pull it through and insert the needle again below the stitch to anchor it in place. Continue working from left to right downwards to form a leaf as shown in the diagram. If you want the leaf to swish to the right, place the anchor stitch to the right. If you prefer it to move to the left, then anchor the stitch to the left. This technique will give the leaf its own natural movement. For wheat and lavender, place your anchor stitch straight down the center.

Satin Stitch

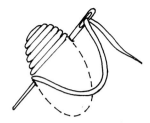

Work the stitches so that they fit closely together. Care must be taken to keep a smooth and straight outside edge. The stitches may be worked straight or slanted. This may look easy, but it takes practice to make it perfect.

Stem Stitch

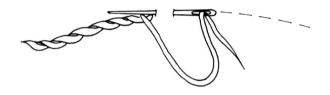

Work from left to right taking regular, slightly slanting stitches along the line of the design, making sure to keep the thread below the needle.

Straight Stitch

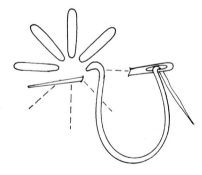

The straight stitch is a single stitch which can be worked in any direction. Bring out the needle at one end and take it down again at the other end.

SILK RIBBON STITCHES

Threading the Needle with Ribbon

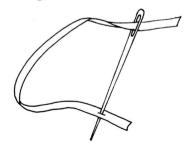

Thread the ribbon through the eye of the needle. Insert the point of the needle back through the center of the ribbon about 5mm (¼") from the end. Pull the long end of the ribbon taut until the ribbon knots on the needle's eye.

Ribbon Stitch

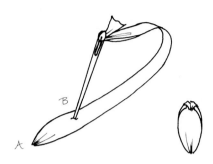

Bring the needle up through the fabric at point A, spread the ribbon flat on the fabric and return the needle back through the center of the ribbon at point B. Carefully pull the needle through to the back of the fabric as the shape of the petal or leaf will depend on the ribbon curling slightly at the tip.

Rose Bud

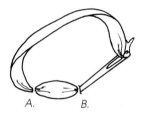

Using a straight stitch, bring the needle through the fabric at point A, and return the needle down at point B. Cover the first straight stitch with a second stitch starting slightly below and returning the needle slightly above the first stitch.

Ribbon Straight Stitch

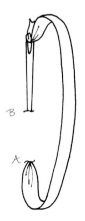

Bring the needle up through the fabric at point A. Spread the ribbon flat and return the needle through the fabric at point B.

Wild Pansy (Johnny Jump-up)

Diagram 1　　*Diagram 2*　　*Diagram 3*

Diagram 4　　*Diagram 5*

This flower is also sometimes called a Johnny jump-up. Work two straight stitches in the shape of a V. Work two smaller stitches overlapping the V (diagram 1).

Work one straight stitch directly below the V. Work two more stitches, one on either side of the first stitch (diagram 2).

To work the center petals, place one straight stitch between the V. Place two more stitches, one on either side of the first stitch. Repeat for the lower petals (diagram 3). Work three or four straight stitches in DMC cotton over the top center petals. Repeat for the lower petals (diagram 4).

To work the calyx, place two straight stitches, one on either side, between the top and the lower petals (diagram 5).

Ribbon Leaf

Cut a small length of ribbon. Fold both ends towards the center, gather the tails together and secure with needle and thread.

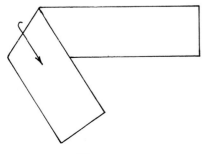

Diagram 1

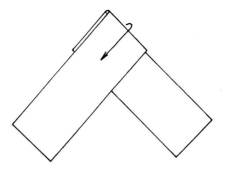

Diagram 2

Diagram 3

Ribbon Rose

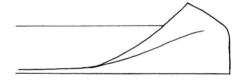

Diagram 1

Fold the ribbon in half widthwise (diagram 1).

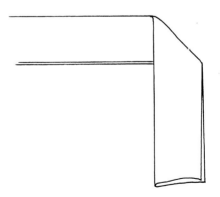

Diagram 2

Leaving a tail of at least 5cm (2"), fold the ribbon at a 90° angle, (diagram 2).

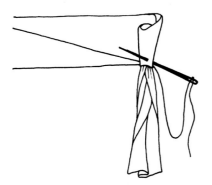

Diagram 3

Commencing at the lower right-hand corner of the angled edge, roll the ribbon several times to the left until the 90° fold has been covered. Stitch to secure the end of the roll (diagram 3).

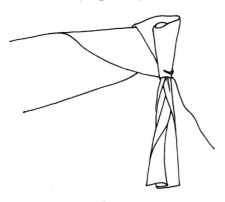

Diagram 4

Fold the top edge of the ribbon back away from the center roll (diagram 4).

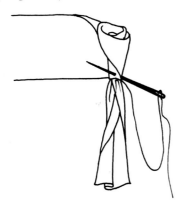

Diagram 5

Roll the center to the left until the fold is covered. Stitch to secure as before (diagram 5).

With the ribbon now at full width, continue to fold, roll and stitch until the rose is the desired size. Cut the ribbon, leaving a 5cm (2") tail (diagram 6).

Diagram 6

Fold the top edge of the ribbon back away from the rose at a 90° angle, (diagram 7).

Gather the tail between thumb and forefinger into the base of the rose. Stitch to secure. Trim the tails back to 1cm (⅜"). Roll the tails together tightly up to the base of the rose, enclosing the raw edges. Stitch to secure (diagram 8).

Diagram 7   *Diagram 8*

Ribbon Rosebud

To make a rosebud, work in the same way as described below for the Ribbon Roses. Stop when the bud reaches the desired size. Secure the tails of the ribbon at the base of the bud in the same manner as the rose.

Field Flower

Work a colonial knot or sew a small bead for the center of the flower. Using a straight stitch, bring the needle up through the fabric close to the center knot or bead. Keeping the silk ribbon perfectly flat, return the needle back through the fabric directly behind the first stitch, leaving a loop the size of the petal required (diagram 1). Work four or five petals around the center in this manner (diagram 2).

Diagram 1 *Diagram 2*

Looped Rose

Diagram 1 *Diagram 2*

Mark a small dot on the fabric for the center of the rose. Thread a needle with 30cm (11½") of silk ribbon and knot the end. Bring the needle up through the fabric on the edge of the center dot. Work a straight stitch 5mm (¼") away from the center dot, leaving a small loop in the silk ribbon. Work three more loop stitches around the center dot forming a cross (diagram 1). Work four more loop stitches between the first four stitches (diagram 2). Stitch a small pearl in the center of the rose.

Stem Stitch Rose

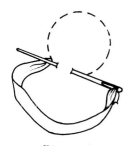 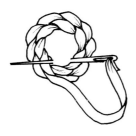

Diagram 1 *Diagram 2*

Draw a small circle onto the fabric. Starting on the outside of the circle, work small stitches in stem stitch, working in an anti-clockwise direction and spiralling inwards until you reach the center of the flower. Loop the thread over the center stitch and return the needle to the back of the work and finish off.

Diagram 3

Tea Rose

Diagram 1

Diagram 2

Diagram 3

Make a small ribbon rose and stitch in place (diagram 1).

Thread a needle with 30cm (11½") of silk ribbon and knot the end. Bring the needle to the front of the fabric as close to the rose as possible. Thread a small needle with sewing thread to match the silk ribbon. Bring the needle to the front of the fabric at the base of the silk ribbon. Using the sewing thread, gather the bottom edge of the silk ribbon for approximately 4cm (1½") (diagram 2).

Pull up the gathers to form a petal. Secure the petal in place by pushing the upper edge of the silk ribbon towards the base of the rose and return the needle to the back of the fabric. Secure with a few backstitches. Repeat until four or five petals surround the rose.

CUSHION MAKING

These directions will assist inexperienced cushion makers to successfully sew up their finished embroidery. Several cushions are in varied shapes so these directions will not apply exactly to every project but the overall ideas for making cushions remain similar.

All seam allowances are 1.5cm (⅝").

Back

Cut two pieces 36cm x 19.5cm (14" x 7¾"). Neaten raw edges. With right sides facing, stitch the two pieces together for a distance of 2.5cm (1") from each end (diagram 1). This leaves a space in the center for the zipper. Press the entire seam open.

Before inserting the zipper, secure the ends of the tape together with zigzag stitching to prevent stress on the seam at the upper end of the zipper (diagram 2).

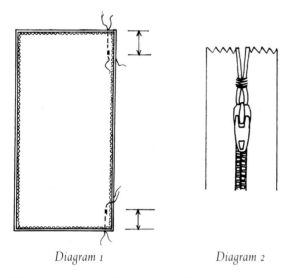

Diagram 1   *Diagram 2*

Place right side of the zipper facing the wrong side of the fabric, align the teeth with the folded edges of the seam opening and position the zipper behind the opening. Pin and tack the zipper in place (diagram 3).

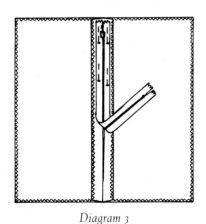

Diagram 3

Machine stitch and press the seam (diagram 4).

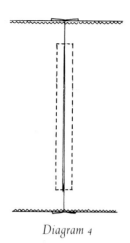

Diagram 4

Piping

Cut strips of fabric 5cm (2") wide on the cross. Join the fabric strips into a continuous length sufficient to cover the required piping cord (diagram 5). Place the piping cord down the center of the wrong side of the fabric strip. Bring the raw edges together, folding the fabric to enclose the piping cord. Using a zipper foot, machine stitch the folded fabric as close as possible to the piping cord (diagram 6).

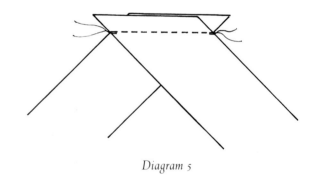

Diagram 5

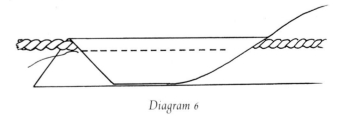

Diagram 6

Square off one end of the piping. Starting half way along one side of the cushion front, pin the piping in place up to the first corner. Carefully clip the two layers of piping fabric to within 2mm (⅛") of the corded edge and fold the piping around the corner (diagram 7). Continue to pin the piping around the cushion front in this manner until you reach your starting point. Cut off the excess piping, allowing 1.5cm (⅝") extra at both ends (diagram 8). Unpick the piping stitching up to 4cm (1½") at both ends.

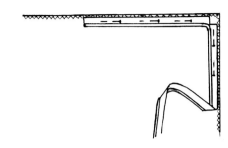

Diagram 7

Diagram 8

With right sides facing, machine stitch the ends of the fabric together. Press the seam open (diagram 9).

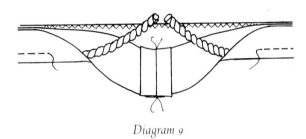

Diagram 9

Cut 1.5cm (⅝") from both ends of the piping cord. Butt the cut ends together and wrap the join with masking tape. Place the piping cord back inside the fabric and stitch again (diagram 10). Using a zipper foot, machine stitch the piping to the front of the cushion (diagram 11).

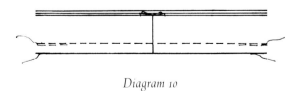

Diagram 10

Diagram 11

Frill

Cut three strips of fabric (see Cutting Layouts). For a more luxurious frill, cut four strips. With right sides facing, join the fabric strips into a continuous length (diagram 12).

With wrong sides facing, fold the frill in half along the length. Stitch two gathering rows along the raw edge of the frill (diagram 13).

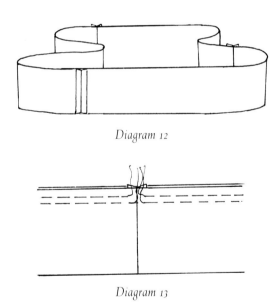

Diagram 12

Diagram 13

Fold the frill into four equal lengths and mark each fold with a pin. Find the halfway point on each side of the embroidered cushion front and mark with a pin. Matching the pins, pin the frill to the cushion front (diagram 14). Pull up the gathers, allowing extra at each corner. Pin and tack in place. Machine stitch the frill to the cushion front (diagram 15).

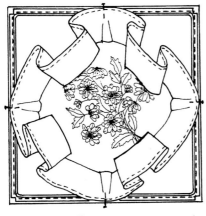

Diagram 14

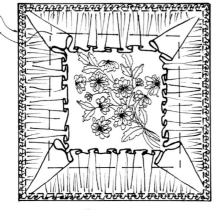

Diagram 15

Attaching the Back

Tack the frill flat against the cushion front to ensure that none of the frill will be caught within the seam. Open the zipper and, with right sides facing, pin and tack the back to the cushion front (diagram 16). Machine stitch, clip the corners and neaten the raw edges. Turn right side out and undo the tacking.

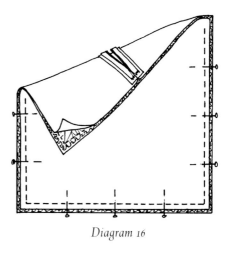

Diagram 16

Cutting Layout

115cm (45")

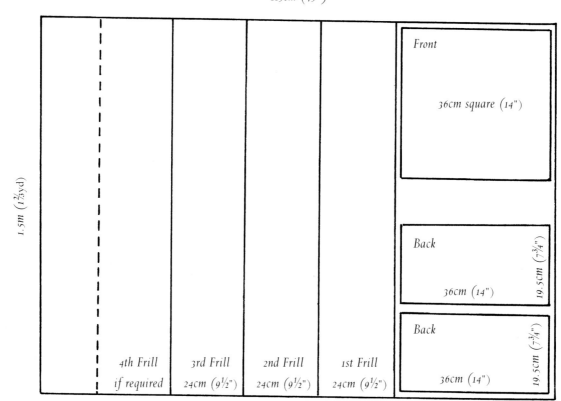

1.5m (1⅔yd)

| Front |
| 36cm square (14") |

| Back |
| 36cm (14") | 19.5cm (7¾") |

| Back |
| 36cm (14") | 19.5cm (7¾") |

| 4th Frill
if required | 3rd Frill
24cm (9½") | 2nd Frill
24cm (9½") | 1st Frill
24cm (9½") |

SATIN BINDING FINISH

A satin binding is used for the blanket projects, these instructions will help you complete your blankets.

Lay the blanket flat with the embroidered side facing upwards. Place the satin binding underneath the left-hand side of the blanket, allowing 3.5cm (1½") binding to overlap above the corner (diagram 1).

Fold the top edge of the binding (A–B) back over the blanket (diagram 2).

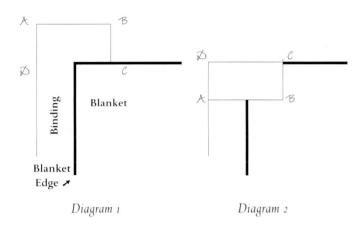

Diagram 1   *Diagram 2*

Fold the top left-hand corner of the satin binding (point D) diagonally across to the edge of the blanket (diagram 3).

Fold the satin binding over the blanket, form a neat 45° diagonal corner piece and then tack into place (diagram 4).

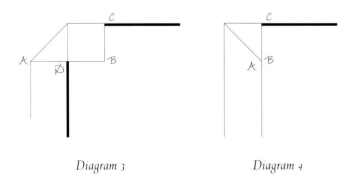

Diagram 3   *Diagram 4*

Carefully position the binding and start tacking around the blanket. At the three remaining corners, fold the binding under to form a 45° diagonal, neatly position and tack into place.

When you reach the top left-hand corner of the blanket, cut off the excess binding, leaving 3.5cm (1½") overlap (diagram 5). Fold the overlap into an arrowhead (diagrams 6a, 6b, 6c).

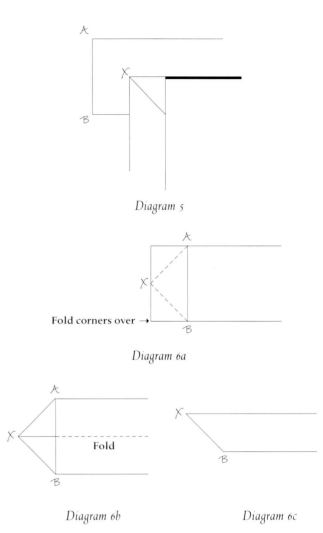

Diagram 5

Diagram 6a

Diagram 6b   *Diagram 6c*

Fold the satin binding over the top edge of the blanket and form a diagonal corner piece, which can be positioned adjacent to the diagonal piece made previously, and then tack into place (diagram 7).

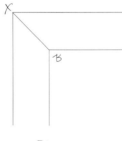

Diagram 7

Hand sew with fine slip stitch, working both the front and back of the corner.

Zigzag your binding to the blanket using the widest zigzag stitch on your sewing machine. Unpick your tacking stitches.

Slip stitch the lace immediately below the binding, gathering it slightly at all four corners.

PATTERNS & DESIGNS

Baby's Coat Hanger page 12

1 square = 2cm (¾")

Increase tracing to 142%

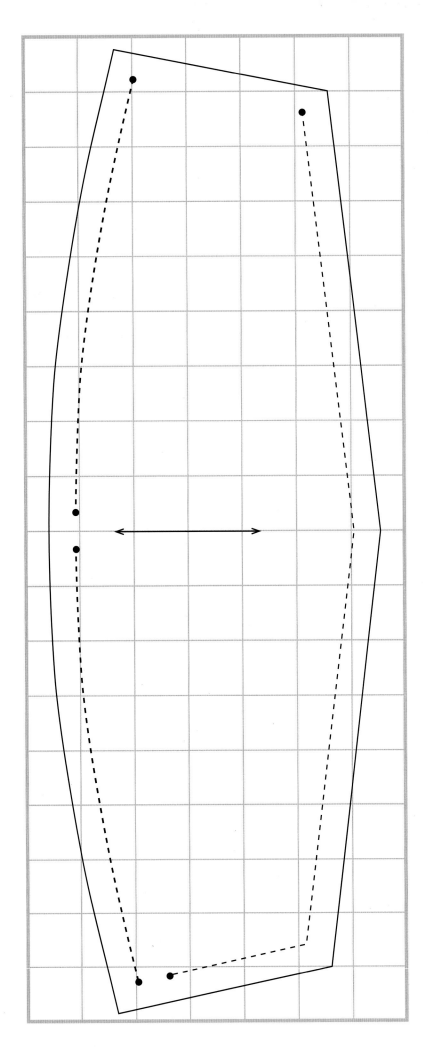

Baby's Jacket page 14
1 square = 2.5cm (1")
Increase tracing to 280%

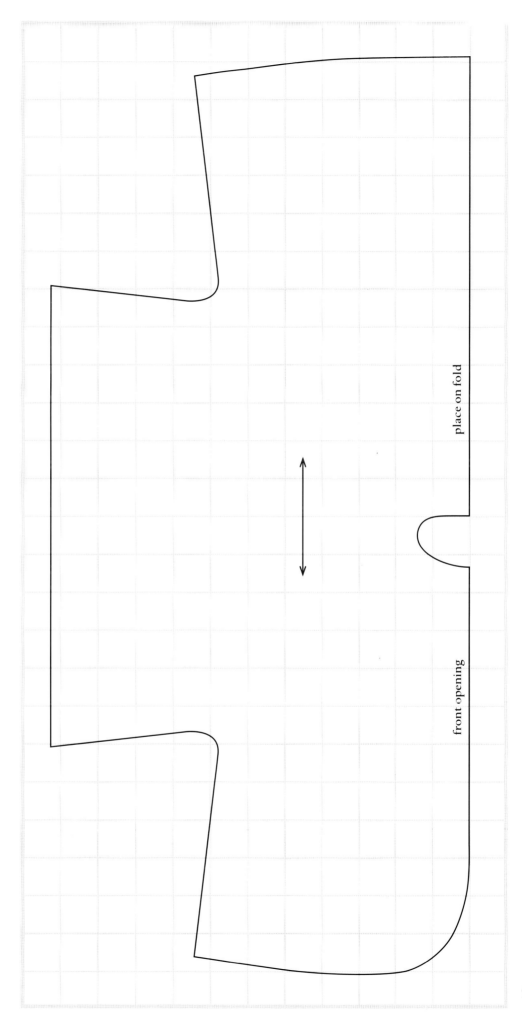

place on fold

front opening

Baby's Romper page 16
1 square = 4cm (1⅜")
Increase tracing to 270%

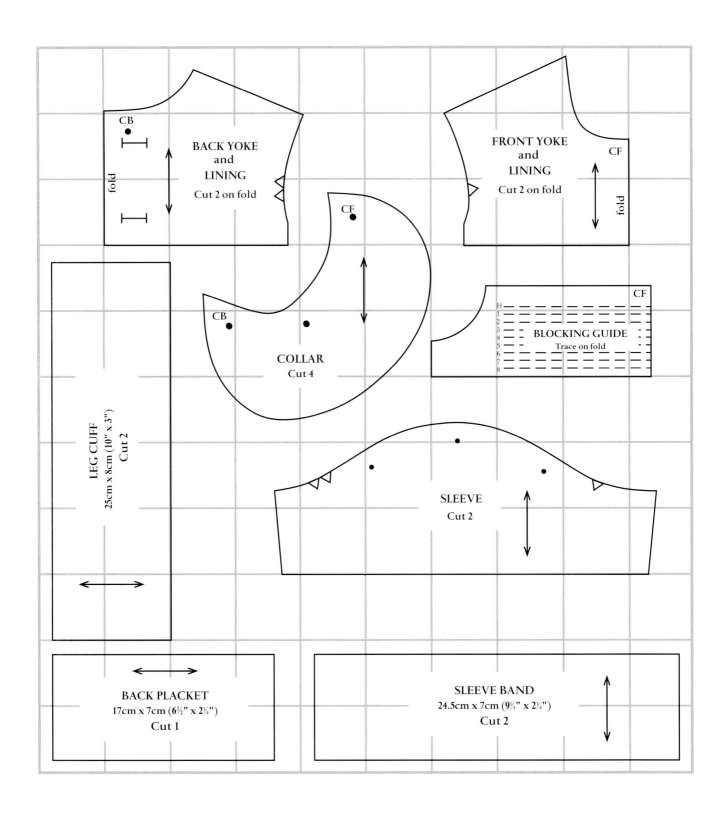

BACK YOKE
and
LINING
Cut 2 on fold

CB

fold

FRONT YOKE
and
LINING
Cut 2 on fold

CF

fold

CF

COLLAR
Cut 4

CB

CF

BLOCKING GUIDE
Trace on fold

H
1
2
3
4
5
6
7
8

LEG CUFF
25cm x 8cm (10" x 3")
Cut 2

SLEEVE
Cut 2

BACK PLACKET
17cm x 7cm (6½" x 2¾")
Cut 1

SLEEVE BAND
24.5cm x 7cm (9¾" x 2¾")
Cut 2

Baby's Romper page 16

1 square = 4cm (1⅜")

Increase tracing to 270%

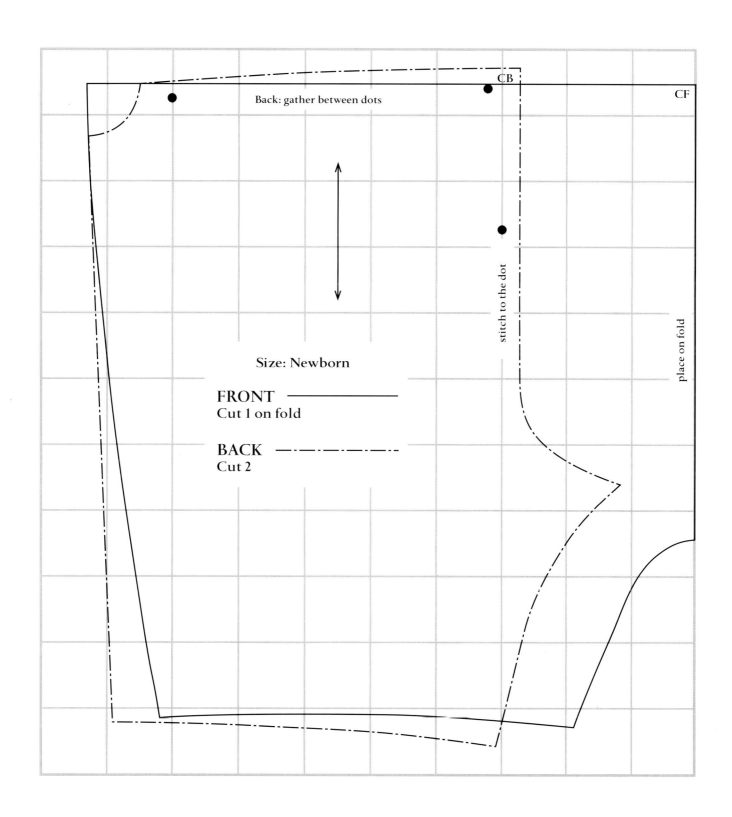

CB

CF

Back: gather between dots

stitch to the dot

place on fold

Size: Newborn

FRONT ———————
Cut 1 on fold

BACK —·—·—·—·—
Cut 2

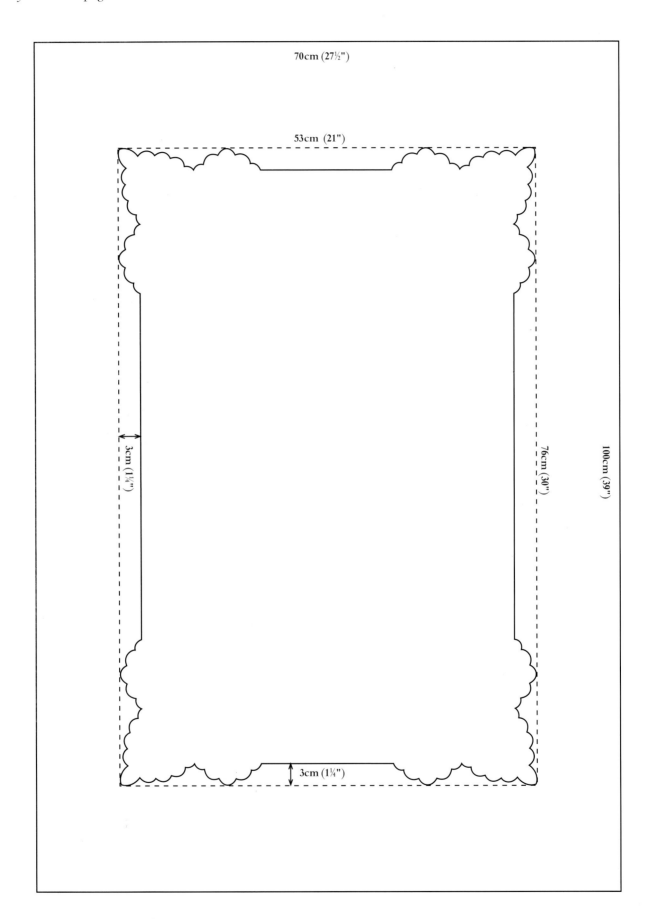

70cm (27½")

53cm (21")

3cm (1¼")

76cm (30")

100cm (39")

3cm (1¼")

Gold Heart Cushion page 28
Heart template: Increase tracing to 200%
Cushion design: Increase tracing to 154%

Old Gold Rose Cushion page 36
Increase tracing to 117%

Flower Spray page 47
Increase tracing to 117%

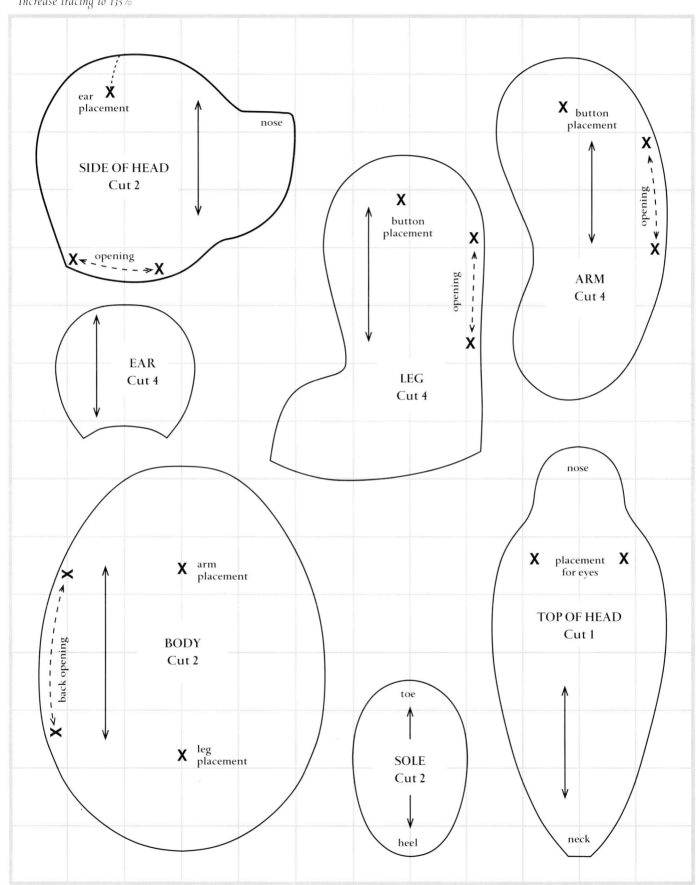

SIDE OF HEAD
Cut 2

ear
placement

nose

opening

EAR
Cut 4

X
button
placement

LEG
Cut 4

opening

X
button
placement

ARM
Cut 4

opening

BODY
Cut 2

X
arm
placement

back opening

X
leg
placement

toe

SOLE
Cut 2

heel

nose

X
placement
for eyes
X

TOP OF HEAD
Cut 1

neck

BED JACKET SCALLOP AND NECKLINE PLACEMENT

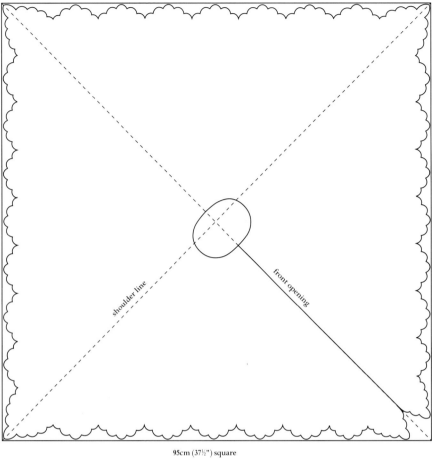

95cm (37½") square

Bed Jacket page 66
Actual size

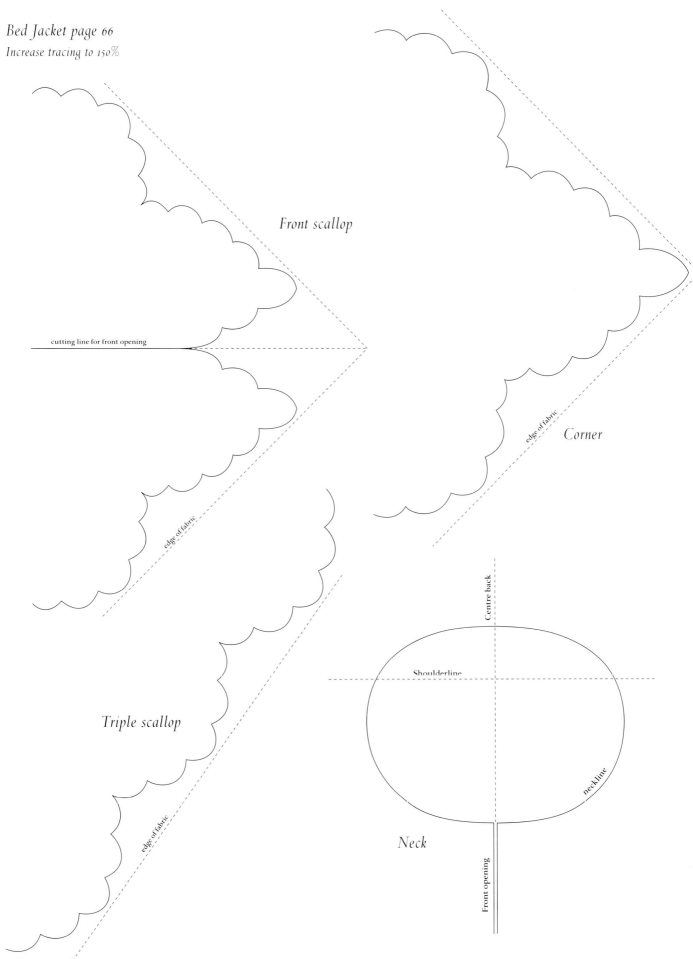

Bed Jacket page 66
Increase tracing to 150%

Front scallop

cutting line for front opening

edge of fabric

Corner

Triple scallop

edge of fabric

edge of fabric

Centre back

Shoulderline

neckline

Neck

Front opening

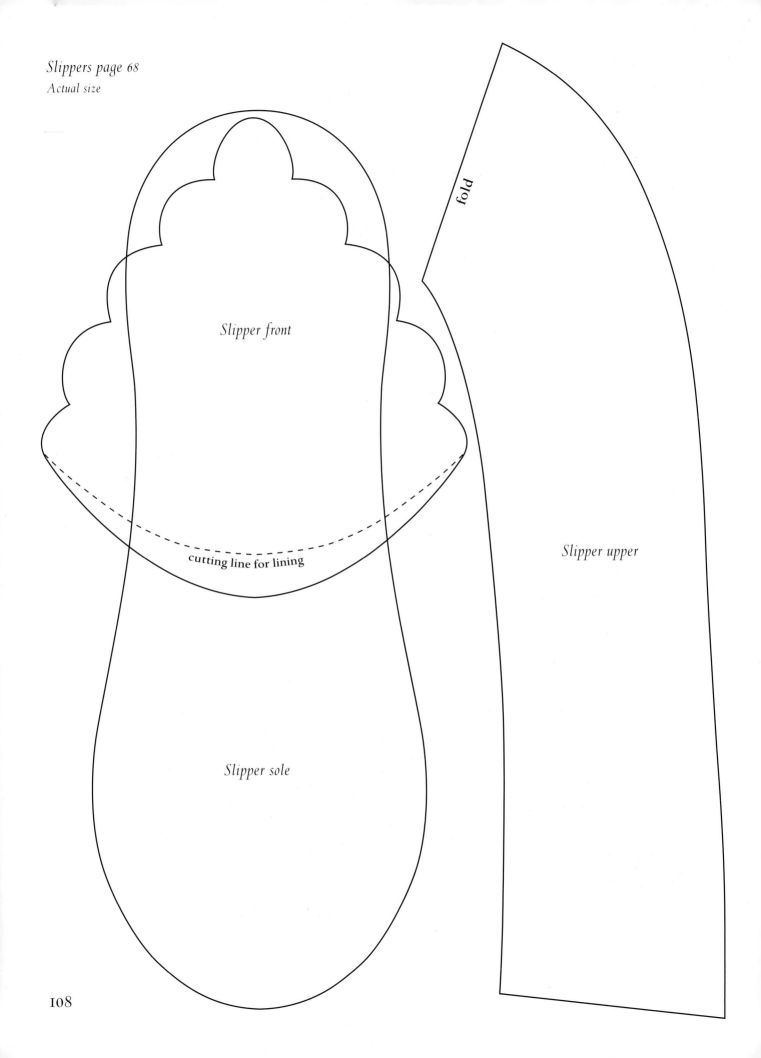

Slippers page 68
Actual size

Slipper front

cutting line for lining

Slipper sole

fold

Slipper upper

108

Heritage Rose Blanket page 72

Small posy of roses and forget-me-nots

Actual size

Heritage Rose Blanket page 72

Large spray of roses and forget-me-nots

Increase tracing to 154%

Victorian Posy Rug page 74
Increase tracing to 154%

The Three Bears page 76
Increase tracing to 154%

III

The Tired Twins page 78

Increase tracing to 156%

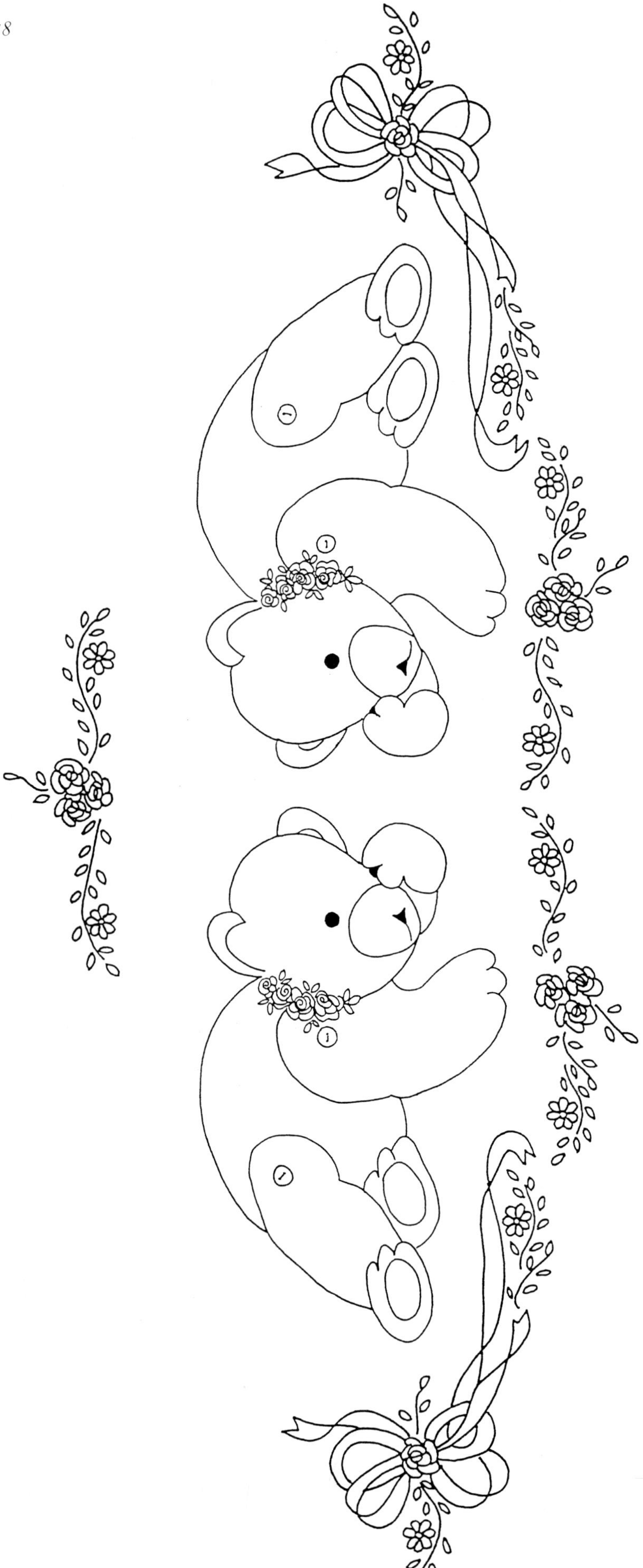